The Dedicated Life of an American Soldier

The Dedicated Life of an American Soldier

Colonel J. L. "Ray" Ramos
U.S. Army (ret.)

Kailua Kona, Hawaii
September 2015

This book was written by Ray Ramos and is based on his memory of events, and of conversations with people from his past and from the present. To the best of his knowledge, the information in this book is true, within the margins of human memory.

The photographs in these pages are copies of official United States Army photographs, with the obvious exception of family photographs.

Quotations from CITIZEN SOLDIERS by Stephen Ambrose are reprinted with permission of Simon & Schuster, Inc. © 1998 by Ambrose-Tubbs, Inc. All rights reserved.

The Dedicated Life of an American Soldier

All Rights Reserved
© 2015 by Ray Ramos

ISBN-13: 978-1508785569
ISBN-10: 1508785562

Printed in the United States

Table of Contents

The Dedicated Life of an American Soldier

Publisher's Note

There aren't many veterans of the Second World War still alive today. But Ray Ramos is not only very much alive, his mind is clear and his memory is sharp.

In "The Dedicated Life of an American Soldier," his autobiography, he first reaches back to his familial roots in the late 19th Century and then recounts vivid images from his early years growing up in the Washington, D.C. area. His personal account of the Great Depression brings a special poignancy to that time.

And in the main of the book, Ray speaks of his military service in Europe as the Allies pushed back against the Nazis. With unerring and powerful detail, he illuminates the humanity, the courage, and the insanity of war. He also reveals important truths about the what really happened in the fight to free Europe, providing valuable insights that have only recently begun to surface.

While Ray wrote his book so that his family should know of their forebears, there is much detail in his account that would be a challenge to find in officials reports. In fact, his story is our nation's history.

Tony Seton
Carmel, California

The Dedicated Life of an American Soldier

<u>Dedication</u>

This story is Lovingly Dedicated to
the late Grace Hardy Ramos,
the mother of our children

Kathleen R. Sharp
Suzanne R. Swanson
Robert L. Ramos
Rosemary R. Macaluso
Grace R. Apfel

The Grandchildren
And
Great Grandchildren

The Dedicated Life of an American Soldier

To Meredith

My best friend, most admired, strongest supporter, my fearless and most honest critic and the one person I most want to please.

I want to express my gratitude for the many, many continuous days on the computer and your encouragement in my behalf. You always worked tirelessly with me to get the job completed.

My remarks here are certainly not limited only to this book but for more than forty years of married life.

May our Blessed Lord continue to shower His blessings on you forever.

The Dedicated Life of an American Soldier

In Recognition

I want to acknowledge the many people who have encouraged, inspired, provided technical support, and in some cases prodded me to write this book.

Mary Pat & Bill Bray
Stuart M. Chudnofsky, M.D.
Esther S. Chudnofsky, RN
Frank DiPaola
J.C. Fry, Maj. Gen. USA (Ret)
Frank V. Gardner, State Dept. Officer
Rosemarie Gardner
Carlton & Grace Hardy
Phillip & Shirley Ladd
George Macaluso
Michael Peter
David & Loree Placeres
Grace H. Ramos
Dan Raymond, Maj. Gen. USA (Ret)
Linda Sue & Joel Reda
Tony Seton, Publisher
Mary Gardner Shannon
Donna Peter Vance

The Dedicated Life of an American Soldier

<u>*Gone But Never Forgotten*</u>

May they rest in peace.

Arland F. Bond, Col. PH

Michael J Cosella, Lt. PH

Jack Davis, Lt. PH, KIA

Jerre Pennell Sgt.

Allison Ware, Capt. PH

Norman Watkins Lt. PH, KIA

KIA - Killed in Action

PH - Purple Heart

The Dedicated Life of an American Soldier

Introduction

Why I Wrote My Story

In the 1950s, 1960's, and 1970's, senior family members and friends suggested and urged me to write the story about my life and military career experiences. I would reply, Yes, maybe someday. Then I thought, Who would be truly interested?"

I am now in the twilight of my life, and all of my senior family members - my dear parents, aunts, uncles, my two brothers Francis Xavier and Ludwood Robert, and my sister Anne Virginia (all my younger siblings are now deceased) and close friends are now with our God. I realized that much of the family history is in danger of being lost forever. I began writing this on and off beginning in the year 2007. This is my story as best I can recall.

I knew a number of my ancestors as a child, and I remember them well when they spoke of their life experiences. Some of the other information came from my sister Anne Ramos Peter who lived her entire life in the Washington, D.C. area. My nephew Michael J. Peter provided valuable information from his own research. Other family data was obtained from the book titled, "The Walshes of Burgundy," by my first cousin Francis Victor Gardner, a former WWII United States Marine, later FBI Special Agent and finally a U.S. State Department diplomat.

My appreciation for much of the historical information goes also, to Frank's daughter, my godchild Rosemarie Gardner and my sole surviving cousin Mary Gardner Shannon, her daughter Mary Patricia Shannon-Bray and her husband Bill Bray.

Thank you to my granddaughter Linda Sue Sharp Reda for introducing and encouraging me to utilize an automatic speech recognition software system in writing portions of this book.

And of course I can never fully express my gratitude to my wife, Meredith Littleton Ramos for her encouragement and for the hundreds of computer hours she contributed in bringing this book to fruition.

<u>My Ancestors</u>

How did we get here? The Ramos side of the family is more difficulty to trace. Since I am the oldest living survivor and I know very
little about my father's relatives. The Great Depression of 1929-1939
precluded vacations and travel for the vast majority of families.

A portion of the Ramos family lived in New York and I only recall
visiting them as a young child. The remainder lived in Puerto Rico. I
am grateful for some background information provided from such
sources as my dad, nephew Michael Peter, and cousin FBI
Supervisory Special Agent Laura J. Ramos.

It is understood that the Ramos' originally came from the Basque
portion of Northern Spain. Political unrest between the Basques, an
ancient Caucasian people, and the rest of Spain likely caused the
family to leave Spain and emigrate to Cuba. After some time they relocated to Puerto Rico. At that time Cuba and Puerto Rico were pos-
sessions of Spain. In Puerto Rico, they settled in what was called the
High Ramos Castilio, overlooking a village identified as the Rosario,
where they had a coffee farm.

After the Spanish-American War of 1898, the United States acquired
Puerto Rico and it became a Commonwealth making Puerto Ricans
U.S. Citizens. The inhabitants all spoke Spanish, as did Dad's family.
When Puerto Rico became a U.S. Possession, all of the Ramos clan
were delighted and very proud to become U.S. citizens.

During WWI the 65th U.S. Infantry Regiment composed of Puerto
Ricans was deployed to the Panama Canal serving as the security
force for the Canal. During that war the concern was that German
naval forces or saboteurs might attempt to damage or destroy the
locks causing commercial/military west coast supplies and U.S.
Naval forces to transit below South America to gain access to the
Atlantic Ocean, the East Coast and Europe. Dad's older brothers

served in that infantry regiment.

My paternal grandfather, Candido Ramos-Sepulvida, became ill with the flu during WWI. The disease was so contagious that many of the corpses were burned in groups in large pits to control or contain the spread of the disease. Out of respect, the older brothers did not want their father's remains burned in a mass grave. They buried Candido in the local Catholic cemetery. I believe this took place before mom and dad knew each other. My paternal grandmother was Antonia Ramos. They were owners of a large coffee farm.

My mother, Margaret Ramos, was the issue of Irish parents and grandparents who traced their roots to Ireland.

At about age 17, my father, Jose Cosme Ramos, enlisted in the U.S. Infantry and was sent to Ft. Bragg, North Carolina. After training he was promoted to the grade of Private First Class. While there he was injured and lost the end joint of a finger. He was sent to Walter Reed General Hospital in Washington, for rehabilitation.

Margaret Elizabeth Bruen and "Rommie," as my mother lovingly called him, met in 1920 at Walter Reed Army General Hospital. She was working there as an Army Field Clerk (a rank like today's warrant officer). Dad was a patient recovering from hand surgery.

During and shortly after WWI, the Knights of Columbus sponsored dances for soldiers. Young ladies would be taken by bus to a military base or facility to dance with the troops. Ladies would sit on one side of the dance floor with the soldiers seated along the opposite wall. When the music would begin the young soldiers would cross the room and ask a lady to dance. And that's how my parents met.

Mother had been dating a young Army doctor at the hospital when she met "Rommie." He was 18 and she was just 20 in 1920. They became engaged and later eloped to Baltimore, where they were married on August 26, 1921 in a local Catholic church. (I am so pleased that the medical doctor did not win my mother's hand and heart!) I arrived on the 29th of August 1922, almost as an anniversary present. Mother was a great teacher and helped dad perfect his language skills. As a child, we only heard English spoken in the family by both parents.

When Dad's Army enlistment was completed, he was honorably discharged. After their marriage both my parents worked. Mother at the

War Department, which now is called the Department of Defense. Dad worked for the Washington Terminal Railroad Company. That national historical building is better known as Union Station. The soft coal powered steam locomotives from all railroads operating in and out of Washington were repaired, overhauled, and returned to service from the large rebuild shops located a few miles from the Capitol. Dad initially worked there as an apprentice machinist and later as a journeyman machinist.

I remember going to the overhaul facility to see my dad. He would put me in a locomotive cab and give me a ride on the turntable, which rotated and would align the engine with different repair pits. It was called the Round House with many repair stalls. Very impressive for me to see my dad operating the locomotive engines.

During WWII the U.S. Navy had an urgent requirement for trained machinists to fabricate large caliber naval guns. Dad answered the call, and worked as a machinist at the Washington Naval Gun Factory. There he developed and perfected a technique to greatly reduce the time in fabrication and assembly of naval guns. In recognition of that accomplishment, he received a monetary award. But far more important in dad's heart was the Navy awarding him the prestigious Navy "E" award of Excellence. Years later President Ronald Reagan honored the memory of "Rommie."

Now let me go back further.

My paternal grandmother, Ana Antonia Ramos-Torres Rodriguez, died in 1923 when I was an infant. All of her sons who resided in the U.S. Mainland returned to Puerto Rico by boat for her Requiem Mass and interment. I remember that my dad and all of his brothers wore a one-inch black arm band as an outward sign of their loss. I can also recall that a wreath would be placed on a residence front door to signify that a death had recently occurred in the family. It was a common practice of all religious faiths in those days. Neighborhood children would not play or make a noise near that location. When a hearse was approaching with lights on, all regular traffic would pull to the side of the road and stop. Male pedestrians wearing hats would remove their hats as an outward sign of respect for the deceased. I had not thought of these practices for some 80 years. I record them here so that family members will realize how our world has changed. It was a much more gentle society then.

Descendants of the Ramos-Bruen union have contributed to the betterment of our nation and its society by providing soldiers in World War I, World War II, and the post-World-War II "Iron Curtain" years. We have also contributed a CIA Spanish language interpreter, professional army officers,, a computer engineer, a Ph.D. in speech therapy, a college professor, a classical pianist, U.S. government executives, a computer forensic examiner, a registered nurse, an electrical contractor, U.S. Coast Guardsman, an environmentalist, an inventor with a U.S. Patent, a machinist, and an iron fabricational artist.

My dear beloved parents are buried in the same plot along with my maternal grandmother and my brother Francis Xavier Ramos. The headstone is inscribed "Together Forever" at the Gate of Heaven Catholic Cemetery in Silver Spring, Maryland.

The Walsh-Bruen Contributors

My great, great maternal grandfather, John Walsh, was married to Bridget Fitzgerald-Walsh. She died when her son, Thomas Walsh, was very young. Later John Walsh remarried and had other children. Our maternal great grandfather, Thomas Walsh, was born in Limerick, Ireland in 1821 and at about age 18 immigrated to the USA aboard the sailing ship Patrick Henry. It is likely that young Thomas left Ireland due to famine and for work. He became an American citizen in 1848 at the age of 27. The ship's planned destination was New York; however, due to severe ocean storms the ship diverted to Boston, Massachusetts.

Later as a successful businessman he became the owner of a large wholesale food business. After some years he sold his Boston business and moved to New York. There he again entered the wholesale food industry, and after a while he met and later married my great maternal grandmother, Mary Ryan-Walsh at St. Paul's Catholic Church on October 16, 1851. That marriage produced six sons and four daughters, one of whom became my grandmother, Anna Cecilia Walsh, born May 9, 1867.

After the Civil War (1865) during a trip in the South, my great grandfather purchased a large 280-acre farm known as Burgundy. A beautiful agriculture and dairy farm, it was there that Mr. Walsh became a gentleman farmer and owner. After this purchase he moved his family to Burgundy, which was located a few miles south of Alexandria, Virginia. My maternal grandmother Anna Cecilia Walsh was born at Burgundy. She was an accomplish pianist and music teacher and later became an executive office manager. I called her "Gram."

In 1897, at age 30, my Gram met and married a writer poet, and author; Edward John Bruen who became the father of my aunt, Marie Teresa Bruen, born 11 July 1898 and died 6 February 1989; she was 91 years old. My mother, Margaret Elizabeth Bruen, born 7 July 1900. Mr. Bruen arrived at Ellis Island in January 1892. He was over six feet tall and became a successful syndicated newspaper columnist. He had six sisters back home in Ireland. Each of them took the habit and became nuns in the Catholic Church devoting their lives to the education of school children in Ireland. While in Ireland, young Edward entered a Catholic seminary for a brief period. However, he later had a change of heart and left the seminary.

Over time my grandfather Bruen became seriously addicted to alcohol. As a result my grandparents separated and neither remarried.

In August of 1920 he resided in the home of then-Vice President Calvin Coolidge, in his capacity as Coolidge's speech writer and newspaper reporter. His reporting also saved the WWI Army hero Sergeant Alvin York from losing his farm in 1921. His syndicated articles were published in newspapers like the *New York Herald,* the *Boston Globe,* and other leading publications of those days.

Unfortunately, he was never able to rid himself of the craving for alcohol, which ruined his life. My grandfather moved to New York where he lived until his death on 20 May 1939, destitute and living in a Manhattan flop house. He is buried in an unmarked grave in Calvary Cemetery, New York. It appears that at times my grandfather would write using the name Breen or John O'Grady; possibly out of shame and to remain anonymous? I would have liked to have met him. My maternal grandmother said that I looked a lot like him.

My mother's sister, Aunt Marie, became my godmother. She married Francis Ivory Victor Gardner, who became my Godfather. He was an Army infantry sergeant and served in France during WWI. He died November 8, 1924, as a result of an accident. The accident occurred when Uncle Frank, a mechanic for Oldsmobile, fell from a Washington Oldsmobile building while installing a radio antenna as a favor to a friend. He had put his weight on the foot he had injured during WWI. He was straddling the corner of the building at the roof, and the gutter was wet, as it had recently rained. He fell three stories. My dad, Jose Ramos, arrived at Emergency Hospital while Francis was still conscious. Francis told Dad to "tell Marie to take care of the children." Shortly thereafter, he slipped into a coma and died three days later, leaving Aunt Marie with three children; Dorothy was two years old, soon to turn three on November 23, and died on August 15, 2000; Frank was one year old, soon to turn two on December 2 and died on June 19, 2010; and Mary was an infant of nine months, having been born on February 7, 1924.

Aunt Marie never remarried. While working she was able to complete her formal education and to take courses in engineering at George Washington University, so that she could better manage her Navy contracting responsibilities. Very unusual for a woman in those days. Prior to WWII she was a civilian employee of the Navy Department Bureau of Ordnance. During the WWII years, she attended Officers Candidate School for WAVES at Smith College in Massachusetts and graduated with the commission of ensign. She returned to the Navy Bureau of Ordnance in Washington, serving in the active Navy Reserve as a WAVE during WWII, and for a short time after the end of the war. She earned the rank of Full Lieutenant (the same grade as an Army captain) in the WAVES reserves.

At the end of WWII, Aunt Marie resumed her civilian Navy career until her retirement. She remained at the Bureau of Ordnance. Her title was Contract Negotiator. She worked on classified Navy Subsurface Ordnance Weapons Systems. One was identified as "Subroc," now unclassified.

In her retirement, she acquired the skill of making her own wine, and when my Dad would visit to fix or repair her Falls Church, Virginia home, she would present him with a bottle of delicious wine. Aunt Marie grew the fruit with which she made the wine. They were great buddies. When Mr. Gardner was on his death bed, Dad promised him that he would always be there for the Gardner family, and he certainly kept that commitment. The Gardner children all called him "Uncle Rommie."

Dorothy Gardner was very fond of our great aunt Leocadia Walsh-

Popkins. Dorothy attended St. Joseph's High School and St. Joseph's College in Emmitsburg, Maryland. When Dorothy was about 20 years old, she became a novice, later received her habit, and took the name of Sister Leo in the Daughters of Charity of St. Vincent de Paul religious order. Their vows were poverty, chastity, obedience and service to the poor. Dorothy, as I always called her, had a Master's degree in math and taught in girls' high schools, teaching algebra, geometry, trigonometry, and calculus. She also was the principal at several girls' high schools.

Francis Victor Gardner, born in 1922, my only male Gardner cousin, died June 19, 2010, at the age of 88. After graduating from St. John's High School in 1940, Frank enrolled at Mount Saint Mary's College, Emmitsburg, Maryland, an all male Catholic college. Like so many young men of his age, WWII interrupted his education. Frank enlisted in the United State Marine Corps and served in the Pacific Campaigns of Saipan, Iwo Jima, and Okinawa, attaining the rank of sergeant. After the war, he returned to Mount Saint Mary's college and completed his education. Frank then became an FBI Field Agent, participating in a number of noteworthy cases.

He had by then married Geraldine "Gerry" Donahue who worked in the FBI Field Office. He was about to become the Special Agent in charge when he realized that would require moving his family, and frequent travel away from home. So Frank went to work at the U.S. State Department in Washington. He retired from the State Department with forty years of government service, which included a few State Department assignments in Mexico and South America. Frank and Gerry were blessed with nine children: Karen, Diane, Maureen, Lorraine, Daniel, Rosemarie (my godchild), Ellen, Nancy, and Thomas. Nancy died at an early age (March 31, 1990). Gerry passed away on June 17, 2009.

Mary Gardner Shannon was a good student like her older sister, Dorothy. After graduating from St. Joseph's High School and taking courses at St. Joseph's College in Emmitsburg, Mary worked in the Navy Bureau of Ordnance, Ballistic Section, computing bomb tables during WWII before aspiring to becoming a nun. While in novice training she became ill and had to return home. The Mother Superior advised Mary that when she regained her health that she could return should she desire. When Mary departed the novitiate, her brother Frank went to Emmitsburg to bring her home. En route, he stopped in Thurmount to buy her some lipstick. What a nice brother.

Later Mary continued her education as a night student at the Georgetown University School of Foreign Service in Washington. At that time women were accepted only as night students. Simultaneously, Francis "Frank" William Shannon, a young "GI Bill" student, was attending Georgetown University School of Foreign Service as a day student. Mary and Frank never crossed paths on the campus of Georgetown University. But they met in the fall of 1950 at the Cathedral Club of St. Matthews Parish in Washington, where they both were taking an Arthur Murray ballroom dancing class. They were married in September 1951. Frank graduated from Georgetown University with a degree from the School of Foreign Service a few months later in January 1952. Frank had served in the Navy in WWII and had a full career with the Navy Department in Washington. Mary and Frank had five children: Brian, Mary Pat, Anne, Kevin, and Stephen.

Mary Gardner-Shannon, her daughter Mary Pat Shannon-Bray, and her husband, Bill Bray provided specific birth and death dates, birth sequences, exact details of my godfather Frank Ivory Gardner's injury and resulting death. Many thanks. I am most grateful.

The Early Years

I was born August 29, 1922. My brother Ludwood Robert – or "Bub" as I called him – was born on March 13, 1924. The twins, Anne Virginia and Francis Xavier , were born on March 15, 1926. We were all born in Washington. I made my first Holy Communion in 1929 at Sacred Heart Catholic Church in Washington.

Praises Can Be Expensive

When I was a little boy of about two or three years of age, I had been completely potty trained and taught to flush the toilet paper down the drain. When I would do that, Mother and Gram would clap their hands and encourage me by saying, "What a good boy you are." Of course I looked forward to their praise. When I saw any trash strips of paper, I would flush them down the drain for more clapping and praise.

One day I saw a strange green piece of paper with an old man's picture on it. It was a $20 paper bill. Yes, You guessed it, not understanding its importance, I flushed it down the toilet! In today's economy, that would be like at least flushing a $100 bill down the toilet. This was in the years leading up to the Great Depression. In 1924, Dad worked in the railroad repair/overhaul yards as a machinist that supported the Union Station Railroad Hub. At that time the normal work week was six days for about $25 a week. Mom worked as an executive program manager prior to retirement in the War Department, today's Pentagon. Her weekly income was also about $25.

On one occasion when combining the family income, my parents suddenly realized that they were $20 short. Then there began a detailed search of the house. Finally in desperation they asked me if I had seen a little green piece of paper that looked like the $20 bill they showed me. I replied, yes, and that I flushed it down the toilet. This time there was no clapping, no back slapping of any kind. Instead, I was given a very detailed explanation of specifically what items were to be deposited in the toilet. Money never!

Our Neighbors

I also remember one of our neighbors very well. Her name was Mrs. Carroll. As a young woman she had traveled extensively abroad, and would visit my Mom and Gram in the afternoon and evenings. Mom and Gram enjoyed hearing of her many journeys. Dad enjoyed reading the evening delivered newspaper. I remember a conversation Dad had with Mom about Mrs. Carroll's visits.

She would go into considerable detail about her travels while Dad was trying to read the *Washington Star* newspaper (no longer published). Dad spoke to Mother asking why Mrs. Carroll had to monopolize the evening with her long-winded stories. He said that she talked far too much when she should be at home preparing her husband's dinner.

After hearing my Father's remarks to Mother, I remembered their conversation and the very next day when Mrs. Carroll came to visit, I promptly made this announcement: "Mrs. Carroll, my Mom and Grandmother like your visits and your stories about ocean liners, and ladies all dressed up to eat fancy food on the ship. But my Dad said that you talk too much." Out of the mouth of babes. As my memory serves me, my childish remarks to Mrs. Carroll did not deter her continued visits.

Quick Thinking

My brother Bub was a sweet little boy, and he was very quick with words. I was about three at this time, and he was eighteen months old. He was also being trained to use the toilet at a very tender age. Sometimes, while we were playing he would stop and tell me that he had to quickly go the bathroom to empty his little bladder. One day while playing he had the urge to go, but the cowboys and Indians were fully engaged and he was sorely needed to help me defend the wagon train. Since he could no longer be denied his bladder's demands, Bub wet his pants. Shortly thereafter my mother came out to see how her two little boys were getting along. She saw Bub in his wet pants. She asked, "Bub, did you wet your pants?" Never at a loss for words, he quickly replied "No! Luis did it." (He always called me Luis.) Through his adult years, if Bub ever made an error he would always insist, "No! Luis did it."

Good Samaritan

My first cousin Mary Elizabeth Gardner was at the Ramos three-story row brick residence at 1816 Ingleside Terrace, Northwest, in Washington. Our maternal grandmother Bruen (Gram) was the only adult in the house at that time. She lived with us until her death on 9 April 1997. Gram cooked and was the babysitter for all the children while our parents were at work.

To preclude little Mary, who was just beginning to take toddler steps, from wandering off or being injured, a portable expandable wooden gate had been installed on the house front door. When the wooden baby gate was extended it formed a series of diagonal shaped diamond openings. Somehow, little Mary managed to get her head locked inside one of the diamonds. A few moments later I saw the problem but being only four or five years old I was unable to free her. By this time she was in breathing distress. I ran to Gram telling her that Mary's face was blue. She was also unable to free Mary.

(Note: The following portion of this event I do not personally re-member. Mary provided the successful sequence of events that were shared with her by Gram.)

Unable to free Mary, our grandmother said, "Oh dear God, help me." Suddenly a black man appeared; he was possibly looking for work. He had big strong hands and was able to free Mary without breaking the gate. Gram said, "Thank you, thank you. Wait a min-ute." She had a $10 bill in the house and went to get it to give to the man in gratitude for what he had done. But when she returned to the porch, the man was gone. When she had composed herself, Gram asked a neighbor couple who had been outside if they had seen the man depart. They had not. When Gram recounted the story many years later. She said that she thought the black man could have been Mary's guardian angel.

An Embarrassing Moment for Dad

Back in the 1920's and 1930's an adult movie ticket cost a quarter. In those days Mom and Dad very seldom could ever justify the extravagance of a movie ticket. However, on this particular occasion they did elect to enjoy a film. It was Sunday afternoon after a big meal. Dad was a very hardy eater, while never fat or overweight, this day he might have overeaten a little.

Mother tells this story about Dad. In those days the theater seats would slide back a little (like on a track) to permit other patrons to pass in front of a person already seated. This gave easy access to others looking for seats, or to exit the row. Unlike today, those films were continuous with no break. When the film came to the part where it was playing when you entered, you normally exited the theater.

After being seated for some time, Dad felt a bit uncomfortable due to the recent big meal. In the darkness he opened his trousers and unzipped his fly. Later in the film two ladies who then had seen the complete film began to leave. They had been seated near the middle of the same row in which Mom and Dad were seated. As the first lady passed in front of Dad, he pushed back in his seat as a courtesy to facilitate her exit. The second lady passed in front of Dad just as he was zipping up his fly. The hem of the dress became entangled in Dad's fly just as he was zipping it up. This action securely locked the hem in the zipper. The theater was dark, the lady was pulling on her dress. People in the rear were calling out, "Down in front." Within moments the uniformed usher came rushing to the scene with flashlight in hand turned on. At this point Mother wanted to find a hole in the floor, jump in and close it after her.

Meanwhile, poor Dad was still struggling with his zipper. Finally the usher took his pocketknife and cut the woman free! After that Dad and Mom went to very few movies. When retold, the story always had family members and friends laughing until there were tears in their eyes.

Pulling Gram's Wagon

Our maternal grandmother "Gram" was a very talented and accomplished pianist who was also a very educated lady. During the Great

Depression, she planted a vegetable garden, growing beans, tomatoes, parsley, mint, and sage, and other food items. She would tie the
mint and parsley into little packages, and fill grocery bags with
them. Then I would get my little red wagon, and with Gram, pull the
wagon to the local meat markets in the "Mount Pleasant" area of
Washington. There she would sell the packages for ten cents or three
packages for a quarter and that money was used to purchase meat,
coffee, sugar, flour and the like. For me it was great fun. I never fully
realized how difficult those times were because everybody was like
us. We were taught to never leave lights on if no one was in the
room. We had an ice box and purchased ice blocks from the ice man.
We picked wild blackberries for desserts.

Blackberry chiggers are very tiny mites that get under the skin causing severe itching. Placing kerosene on the affected area killed the
chiggers. That was a minor annoyance in exchange for blackberry
pie!

The Great Depression (1929-1939)

Life for the majority of people during the Great Depression was a
test of will, family commitment, courage, and adaptability. In 1929 at
the start of the Great Depression I was then seven years old. We
lived in Washington for the next four years.

I remember people selling apples on the street corners for a nickel
each. Other people sold pencils, and children sold the evening newspapers on the street corners. Sometimes a man would knock on the
back door, and ask if he could work (cut the grass, paint - whatever)
for lunch because he was hungry. A sandwich and water would do. I
doubt if welfare existed then. People in dire need were helped by
family members and churches. When necessary relatives would take
the children into their homes until the parents were again self supporting. As I reflect back, my siblings and I were very fortunate to
have both parents who had meaningful and lifelong careers. The
Ramos children were not negatively impacted by the Great Depression. We were all happy and knew that our parents worked very
diligently for our well being.

During those times all shoes were made of leather. When we wore a
hole in the sole, we inserted cardboard over the hole. Worn down

heels were switched by Dad to the opposite shoe to obtain even wear and full use. Frayed shirt collars and cuffs were removed, turned around, or reversed and stitched back in place.

Downsizing

My parents had purchased a three-story brick row house in the early 1930's. Due to illness, financial demands, and loaning money to relatives that couldn't be promptly repaid, together with the size of the family (parents, four children, our maternal grandmother) and a government-mandated reduction in salaries, my parents lost their home. We then moved from the three-story house to the house next door, but renting the first floor only.

Thrifty Smoker

Dad smoked in those days. Being thrifty, as did the vast majority of the male population, to save money, he had a little hand-operated machine that permitted him to make his own cigarettes. He purchased pipe smoking tobacco and cigarette papers to make his own smokes. To keep from crushing or having perspiration damage them, he used a metal Prince Albert Pipe Tobacco pocket-size tin container to protect them. The packet fit snugly in his breast overall pocket. The smallest saving was very important in those days.

Moving to Virginia

A couple of years later, suffering some more financial problems, we moved to the 160-acre family farm known as Clifton Dairy Farms across the Potomac River in Fairfax County, Virginia, not far from George Washington's mansion at Mount Vernon. Mom and Dad purchased from her Aunt Leo and Uncle Lud three undeveloped farmland acres. They used Uncle Lud's farm hands to dig the cellar area with a team of horses using a "Drag Bucket." They then built a little two-bedroom, living room, dining room, kitchen and one-bathroom house.

On the farm, Bub and I wore overalls and went barefoot much of the summertime. Bub and I milked the cows, cleaned the barn, fed the pigs, gathered the eggs and did all sorts of other farm chores. The word "allowance" was completely foreign to our understanding.

Mom and Dad took Anne to school at St. Mary's Academy in Alexandria, Virginia, dropping her off on their way to work in Washington. There was no school bus so Bub and I walked to the public grammar school, which was almost two miles away. In my senior grammar school year, I was elected class president and president of the student body. Albert Cox was class vice president. During the May Day festivities. I crowned the May Queen; I don't remember her name. The blonde girl to the left of the May Queen is Mary Murphy. Her dad was a sergeant in the Virginia Highway Patrol. I was very bashful, and had a crush on her. I thought she was very cool.

Our "Aunt" Belle Jeffery

Shortly after the Civil War in 1865 and the purchase of the Burgundy Farm Estate by my maternal great-grandfather Walsh, an unexpected new member of the Walsh Family arrived on the scene. My great grandmother, Mary Ryan-Walsh, was returning to Burgundy Farm from a trip to Alexandria, Virginia in her horse-drawn buggy. Some miles from the farm on a gravel road she saw a little black girl, not ten years old, walking along the dusty road, carrying a few clothes in a bundle. My great grandmother stopped the buggy and asked the little girl where she was going. The girl responded "Dear Lord, I don't know, but Missah Lincoln done freed us slaves, and now I is free." At that, Mary Walsh told her to get in the back of the buggy and that she could work in her Burgundy Farm Home. The little girl said that her name was Belle Jeffery.

A few years later my maternal grandmother, Anna Cecilia Walsh, was born and Belle became her nanny, bathing, feeding, and diapering her. Thirty three years later in 1900 when my mother, Margaret Elizabeth Bruen, was born, "Aunt Belle" was her nanny. When I was born in 1922, Aunt Belle took care of me as well. Aunt Belle was likely 67 years old when I was born.

(The foregoing family events were told to me by both my grandmother Mrs. Anna C. Walsh-Buen and my mother. The following history reflects an experience I clearly remember first hand.)

I remember Aunt Belle very well. She was very dark of skin, possible five feet tall, slim of statue and had only a few teeth that showed when she smiled. She was a very good cook. She had her own bedroom in the main farm house adjacent to Aunt Leo and Uncle Lud's bedroom.

One day when I was seven or eight years old, at my maternal great aunt Leocadia Walsh-Popkins and great uncle Ludwood's Clifton Dairy Farms, I asked my Aunt Belle to fix for me a slice of bread with butter and sugar on top. She did, and I went to the nearby swing under an oak tree. In short order the birds began eating the crumbs that I had thrown about near the swing. I went back into the house and asked Aunt Belle for another slice of bread as before. Aunt Belle said to me, "No, child, I saw you feeding those birds. Dem birds can find their own food. Bread, butter, and sugar is food for folks."

Obviously I did not realize the influence or command authority delegated to Aunt Belle many years before I was born. I said "Dear Aunt Belle, you know that you work here." I had no sooner completed the sentence when my father was pulling down my pants and shorts. He put me over his knees and began spanking me, all the while telling me that when Aunt Belle tells you something it's the same as if your mother or I or your Aunt Leo or Uncle Lud was talking to you. The dear ole Aunt Belle said, "Missah Joe, he don't mean no harm." It was then that I realized just how special Aunt Belle was.

A few years later Aunt Belle became ill and shortly thereafter she passed away. There was a special room in the farm house called "the parlor." It contained the best furniture, heavy drapes, a nice rug on the floor, and a number of ornamental jars that were full of dried rose petals. It was a room used only for special occasions like weddings, funerals, or other special events. Aunt Belle was laid out in the parlor and accorded the highest respect and love from all family and friends who came to mourn her passing. Aunt Belle was the first person to die that I knew. I was not tall enough to see her in her coffin, but I understood that I'd no longer see that "family member" again.

Our Farm Hands

On the farm there was a "bunk house" several hundred yards from the main house. Four young single black farm hands lived there. Our Aunt Belle prepared their food and they had their meals on the porch adjacent to the kitchen. Aunt Belle chewed tobacco as did the hired hands. When they could, they would steal some of her tobacco. Aunt Belle outsmarted them by pouring kerosene over her chewing tobacco. I remember asking her how she could handle the taste. She replied they could not tolerate the taste but it was okay with her. Hired hands were paid $6 or $7 a week, depending on skill and years of service.

A Near Disaster

While living on the farm, we had a creek that was located in the woods about half a mile behind our house. On a frozen winter day, I was about twelve, Bub ten, and Anne eight. Bub and I decided to check the creek for the thickness of the ice. It was an "all boy" thing. Anne insisted on tagging along with us. We told her not to come. When we noticed that she was following us we told her to go back to the house. She was in her snow suit and we were wearing heavy black sweaters. My little sister was always strong-willed. Anne was an original woman's libber, and at such a tender age!

There was a fallen tree that barely spanned the creek. It was then covered with ice and show. Bub and I ran across the tree bridge without incident. When Anne tried to follow us, she slipped and fell into the ice-covered creek, breaking the frozen surface and falling into the water. She was quickly freezing, her little teeth were chattering, and she needed help.

Bob and I rescued her and got her on the bank, discovering that her snow suit and hair were almost frozen. We took her snow suit off, putting her arms thru the sleeves with the "trunk" of my sweater up around her waist. Then we took Bub's sweater and put her legs through his sleeves and the body of the sweater around her middle. We took turns carrying her back to the house.

Bub and I had recently raised two little pigs to maturity. We called them "Mae West" and "Jean Harlow" after two movie queens of that period. The pigs had been slaughtered and the pig pen was clean. We did not want the maid, Cary Jones, to know what had happened since we knew that she would tell our parents. So we put Anne in the pig pen and I went into the house to get clean and warm clothes for her.

After redressing Anne we took her into the house, not realizing that Cary would immediately see the wet hair and change of clothes. Since Anne was the only girl and the apple of my dad's eye, I knew that I was in trouble since I was the oldest and responsible for my younger siblings.

That evening after Dad had been briefed by Cary Jones of the pig pen incident, he said that we had saved our little sister and that was okay. However, in the future we had to be very careful about her safety. Whew!

Sending the Wrong Messages

In connection with our Boy Scout training, Bub and I learned the Morse telegraph code. The Navy had code operators who would send classified messages or orders using special lights from ship to ship. Bub and I decided to use a mirror to flash a message to our Great Aunt Leo as she was driving up Popkins Lane a half-mile away in her Essex automobile. Unfortunately, we did not appreciate that shining the big mirror's sun reflection blinded her. She talked to our dad, and that was the end of "message sending."

Having Friends in High Places

The Washington Terminal Railroad Company performed major steam locomotive overhauls in the Washington area. Their senior executive was known as the Master Mechanic. He had a son my age who liked to visit Bub and I in the summertime on the farm. At that time, a favorite penny candy was called a "jawbreaker." About half the size of a golf ball, the jawbreaker had many different color layers of candy, and was so hard that you could not crack them with your teeth. It had to be sucked.

Bobby Boucher was our friend's name. As little boys Bub, Bobby, and I all slept in the same bed. On one particular occasion our mother came into our bedroom to tell us goodnight. She noticed that none of us responded to her greeting. We all had jawbreakers in our mouths. Bub and I quickly put ours under the white bed sheets. The result was beautiful colors all over the inside of the sheets. Since Bobby's dad was the number one railroad executive, we were not punished. However, after he departed, we were then the recipients of clear new house rules. No more candy or jawbreakers in bed! Mom had not been fooled for a moment!

My Very First Paying Job

U.S. Highway One, then a two-lane blacktop paved road, was about two miles from our house on the farm. A man named John Droder and his wife operated a Chevron gas station there. They offered me a job after school and on Saturdays paying me three cents an hour pumping gas into a large glass bowl at the top of each gas tank. It had graduations from one to five gallons. The customer could see the fuel volume. The gas then went directly into the vehicle tank on a gravity feed. Every station was "full service," which included washing all windows, checking the water level in the radiator, checking the battery and engine oil level, and, of course, the air pressure in all tires, including spare. At that time gas was nineteen cents per gallon, or ninety-five cents for five gallons. On Saturday Mr. Droder paid me a quarter for eight hours since I worked so diligently. I was delighted. In the summer I worked for him six days a week. Sundays were church and family days.

World War I Veterans Bonus

About 1936 a very unusual event took place in our nation. At the conclusion of WWI in 1918, the U.S. government agreed to give those soldiers who fought in that war, a soldier's bonus to be paid in 1945. However, due to the deep depression the veterans needed help in 1932. Seventeen thousand veterans converged in the Washington area during May through July 1932. Many with their wives and children. President Herbert Hoover ordered them off federal government lands, particularly the areas around the Lincoln Memorial and Washington Monument where the veterans had erected tents, shacks, and other shelters for themselves and their families.

A week or so before the President's order, I accompanied my dad when he went to our farm garden and loaded the car with corn, tomatoes, beans, apples, and canned items that my mother had put up for our winter use. She donated many of those items to the veterans. I was very impressed to see their sorry condition, and to talk with some of the veterans and their families. I will never forget their sad plight. Sanitary conditions were extremely meager. Because I was only ten, I was too young to understand the significance of the financial, political, and limited sanitary conditions impacting the entire situation.

President Hoover ordered General Douglas MacArthur to use infantry and cavalry from nearby Ft. Meyer, Virginia to disperse the bonus marchers and then to destroy the tents, shacks, and lean-to's. There was much criticism about using MacArthur since he had commanded in combat the 82nd Infantry Division in WWI. Among many of the veterans there were men who had fought in his units. Ultimately, Congress ordered the bonuses paid in 1936,

Early Schooling

As youngsters, we were taught to have a strong love of country by our parents. Accordingly, my interest in history and the protection of the nation were instilled in me not only by our parents, but in school as well. For the high school years the Ramos family moved back to Washington, so that we could attend Catholic Schools. Bub and I attended the Christian Brothers St. John's High School and participated in the Junior ROTC (Reserve Officer Training Corps) Cadet Program. Bub and I were Cadet Lieutenants in our senior years. Bub was also a member of the rifle team and won a medal for his shooting skills.

A New President and Currency Reform

I was eleven years old when shortly after he took office in his first term in 1933, President Roosevelt closed all of the banks. At that time the country was on the gold standard. That meant that every dollar in circulation and every dollar being printed was backed by gold deposited in the National Treasury at Ft. Knox in Kentucky. Later the president called in all gold in circulation, and we went off the gold standard. The banks were closed and people had to depend on their cash on hand and their coming salaries to get by. Many banks never reopened and the depositors lost their money. Years later the government began to insure deposits. This guarantee remains today and is up to $250,000. We then had currency backed by silver deposits. That money was printed as Silver Certificates. Very few of those bills are still in circulation today because collectors have pretty much bought them up.. They can still be purchased thru collectors for a premium price. Today's U.S. currency is only backed by the faith people have in the government. However, foreign countries and investors are still interested in purchasing our currency.

A Humorous Family Story

(This is a little story told to me by my dear grandmother "Gram" Bruen. It's about her oldest sister and it took place after the civil war at the family estate known as "Burgundy.")

As was the custom of that time, if a young man wanted to court a young lady, he first had to ask permission of her father to pay a visit to her at her home, to chat and have coffee and cake. Always under the watchful eye of a female relative. My great grandfather Walsh knew that a particular young man's family was well respected and established, and said that their son was welcome to visit his daughter.

The day of the visit his daughter (my great aunt) was extremely nervous since this would be the very first time that a gentleman would be calling on her. As evening drew near she had an upset stomach and she experienced gas pains. As she began dressing and "primping," the more nervous she became, and the more intense were the gas pains. That evening she went downstairs, and from the darkened parlor she looked out the windows and could clearly see the long grand approach road. No horseman was in sight. She passed gas and exclaimed, "What a relief." She then went back upstairs to check her hair and appearance. Then she went back downstairs, looking out to see if a rider was in view. She passed more gas. Then she decided to light the coal oil (kerosene) lamp, there in the far corner she saw the young gentleman who had been sitting in the dark. Upon seeing him, she said, "Oh, how long have you been here?" He replied, "Ever since the first relief." He promptly departed, never to return.

I used to think about that story, and in later years wondered if it really was the older sister. Could it have been my dear Gram?

My Teenage Years

My first (freshman) high school year (1937) was spent as a student in St. Mary's Academy in Alexandria, Virginia where I was taught by Holy Cross nuns. The economy was greatly improved by then, and Mom and Dad truly wanted Bub and me to be taught by Christian Brothers during our high school years.

Accordingly, the 1938 school year found us back in the District, as Washington, D.C. was called, living at 5510 9th Street N.W. Anne was enrolled at Sacred Heart Academy high school operated by nuns. She graduated in 1944. Bub, a freshman, and I as a sophomore at St. Johns High School on Wisconsin Avenue. St. Johns was operated by the Christian Brothers, an order of teachers founded by St. John the Baptist De LaSalle in France. St. Johns was a Class 55c Junior, Reserve Officers Training Corps School. It was mandatory that all students participated in the ROTC training. We wore a cadet uniform to class and trained three days of each school week. We closed the street and trained in that area. Based on written tests in our senior years, both Bub and I earned the Cadet Rank of Lieutenant, My first cousin Francis Victor Gardner was in my graduating class of 1940, and he also graduated with the rank of Cadet Lieutenant. More about Frank later.

Bub and I had a buddy named Francis Joseph Peter. "Pete" was in the class of 1941 and Bub in the class of '42. Pete graduated as a Cadet Captain in charge of all government issued weapons. We always thought that Pete was our buddy and his friendship was only with us guys. All the time our little sister was growing up to be a very pretty young lady. But more about that later.

During my high school years in Washington, most working class families lived in brick row houses. There were five or six boys of my age living on our block. Without their parents' permission, they would sneak cigarettes and smoke in the alleys in rear of the homes. I did not like smoking, however, to be one of the boys, I tried it.

At that time my father realized that a couple of his cigarettes were missing. Later one evening he said to me, "Son, bring me my package of cigarettes on the table." When I did, he mentioned the missing cigarettes. He said, "I know that you have been smoking. If you want to smoke, do it with me, but don't give them to your friends since their parents might object." I promptly told the guys that I could smoke with my dad on the front porch. That very next evening they all walked past our house. When I saw them coming, my dad was already smoking and reading the evening newspaper. I quickly lit up and watched their eyes in disbelief. My father was a very wise man. From that day forward I never smoked, That was likely in the year 1938 - long before medical science determined the danger of smoking. Thanks, Dad.

The Perils of Alcohol

A year or so later, the same guys had graduated to alcohol. I knew where Dad kept his whiskey. So, I put a chalk mark on the bottle and shared "a shot or two" with the guys. I did not like it at all! Then I carefully refilled the bottle with water to my chalk mark. Dad normally had a shot of whiskey before dinner. The evening after the whiskey bottle water refill, Dad said, "Son, you have been giving my whiskey to your buddies and replacing it with water. You ruin good whiskey by doing that." Like the time before with the cigarettes, he said, "If you think that you are old enough, have a shot with me. Not behind my back." So I had the shot with my dad in front of my friends walking nearby and that was the end of my whiskey experimentation. Thanks, Dad, for your very wise and loving care.

The Changing Times

As young teenage boys in the Washington summertime, Bub and I would look for lawns that had not been cut for several weeks. That was an indication that there likely was not a young male person in resident. With our push lawn mower, rake, and hand edging tools we would ring the doorbell and offer our services. Sometimes it resulted in negotiations and eventual work. Another way to make money was to recover discarded glass Coke, Pepsi, 7up, larger ginger ale and other bottles. The food markets would pay two cents for all Coke size bottles and a nickel for the larger bottles. Plastic containers for such beverages were not yet in use. It was an easy way to make money.

It seemed like everybody of all Christian faiths went to church on Sunday. For that event all family teens, together with the entire households, attended church. Men wore suits, ties, and hats. In the pews there were hat storage spring-activated catches that men used to free their hands for praying, singing, and following the prayers and music. All ladies wore their best hats, dresses, silk stockings, leather high heels shoes and gloves. When a close family member died, the remaining adult male family member would have a one-and-a-half-inch black band sewn to the overcoat sleeve or suit jacket sleeve for a year. Mourning and prayers for the deceased with reciting of the Rosary was in the evenings with all family members participating.

None of the houses had air conditioning. The only air conditioning I remember was in theaters, large hotels, and upscale department stores. In summer it would be so hot that people found it better to be on the large government lawns in the Washington Monument area, the Lincoln Memorial or the Reflecting Pool. Farmers would bring trucks loaded with cold watermelons. A family would purchase a large melon for a quarter, cut it into slices and use the fruit as a treat and to cool themselves. The little kids would be in their pajamas and sleep on newspapers spread out on the grass. That was how we kept cool.

As a high school student I worked at three drug stores. Not a chain but stores owned and operated by one druggist. His name was Dr. Dingleman. I worked after school and on Saturday and sometimes Sunday afternoon and evenings.

In those years (long before Martin Luther King) there were public drinking fountains and toilets marked for "whites only" and adja-cent or nearby similar facilities for "colored." This was in the Washington area and throughout the South. From what I under-stood, that did not apply in the Northern States.

When I first went to work for Dr. Dingleman he made it clear to me that if I should ever have a black person at the soda fountain who asked for a Coke, never serve it in a glass. Dispense the Coke in a paper cup. Well one day a well-dressed black man went to the soda fountain. There he ordered a Coke. When the druggist heard his order he immediately came to the soda fountain and said to me that he would take care of that customer. He took a paper cup and filled it with ice and Coke. The black man said "I will not drink my Coke from a paper cup." The druggist without a word poured the contents from the cup into a regular Coke glass and gave it to the customer. The man at the fountain enjoyed his Coke and when he finished and put the glass on the counter the druggist took the glass, broke it, and put the pieces in the trash. All the while, the white customers were watching with interest, of course. The black man then departed the store without a word. That is the way it was then. If a black ordered a sandwich, it was placed in wax paper and put in a bag, not consumed at the soda fountain or booths.

Pre-World War II Military Policy

The United States Armed Forces were also segregated. In the Navy, blacks and Filipinos were relegated to jobs as cooks and waiting on officers tables aboard ship. In the Army, blacks loaded cargo, and were organized into Quartermaster Labor Battalions. Segregated for the most part, they were led and commanded by white officers. It was my experience that black officers served in all-black units.

Military Training

While attending Catholic University as a freshman engineering student in 1941, the United States Army had a four-year summer training program called the Civilian Military Training Corps (CMTC), which took place at various regional army stations. The programs were identified as Basic (1st year), Red (2nd year), White (3rd year) and Blue (4th year). I was being trained by the 6th Field Artillery Battalion on their 75 mm artillery guns at Fort Hoyle in Maryland.

There were several hundred CMTC candidates. At the conclusion of each summer encampment a significant number of applicants were eliminated from further training. Those of us who "made the cut" were the troops whom ROTC officers trained, and gained their command experience in times of peace. At the end of my second year, I was awarded a CMTC Medal and was therefore eligible to return for the third-year course. At the successful completion of the Blue 4th year course, a graduate would appear before a board of officers for evaluation, and if found qualified would be awarded a Reserve Officer's commission as a second lieutenant.

Due to Hitler's Nazi expansion in Europe, President Roosevelt federalized the National Guard. Since the National Guard had to be issued the limited weapons, uniforms and training facilities, the CMTC programs were unfortunately terminated.

With dangerous war clouds looming over the free world, our government recognized the need to attract young college graduates into the armed forces. Accordingly, recruiters went to colleges to sign up the then graduating classes as second lieutenants in the Army and Marine Corps, and as ensigns in the Navy. The following year, the same recruitment program was employed. Those graduates, lacking specialized ROTC abilities, were quickly trained in those particular requirements. There was no U.S. Air Force then. They were part of the U.S. Army Air Corps all during World War II.

Shortly after federalizing the National Guard, a selective service draft was instituted. Draft boards from every city and town selected men for military service. Basis for draft exemption were factors such as marital status, age, job skills, and number of dependents. Draft quotas were established for each draft board depending on total population size.

Rationing coupons were required to purchase things like shoes, auto tires, gasoline, appliances, coffee, and sugar. Production of cars ceased. Those factories then produced tanks, aircraft, and other essential military hardware. Cities also had collection points where people would donate aluminum and iron pots, and other critical metals to support the expected war effort. There were no silk stockings for women since silk/nylon was diverted to parachute production.

The government sold war bonds to finance the war for $18.75 which were redeemed after the war for $25 each. Children collected scrap metal used to produce aircraft, tanks, and other weapons. The entire nation supported the war effort. Women took over men's jobs since most able-bodied men were in the military services. Most young single women would not date young men not in the service of their country. They would say my brother, uncle, father, or other family member is in the service, so why not you?

Since Europe was in flames with Germany annexing Austria into the Third Reich and invading France, Belgium, Czechoslovakia, and Poland, it was only a matter of months before WWII would be in full swing. The only opposition in front of Hitler was the British Empire and the Soviet Union. The German invasion of England was expected at any time. Accordingly, in anticipation of the later United States involvement leading to total war, I decided to gain some practical engineering field experience. This was accomplished by working full time for the U.S. Army Engineer District in the office of the Washington Surveyor. At the same time I enrolled as a night student at George Washington University in Washington.

An Unexpected Military Career

I am very sure that my commitment to the security of the United States of America is typical of the millions of other young men and women who in the past, present, and, God willing, in the future, will insure the existence of our beloved and wonderful land. They are all my brothers and sisters regardless of their race, creed, politics, grade, national origin or branch of military service. I was fortunate serving in what I call the "Soldier Army." My career predominantly was served with combat units.

During my WWII service, the Army operated with two distinct major sub-divisions. The first was composed of the Infantry, Artillery, Armor, and Combat Engineers, which I referred to as "The Soldier Army" or "The Fighting Army." The other major elements were the Quartermaster, Chemical, Signal, Medical, and Logistical Commands. These soldiers performed vital tasks in the U.S. and overseas, such as operating military posts, camps and stations, and hospitals; delivering supplies forward, evacuating wounded, operating prisoner of war facilities, and myriad other much needed tasks, normally behind the line of enemy contact.

All of my military service was performed prior to the integration of female troops. In my troop duty experience, I never saw any female military personnel except for two female officers who were my classmates at the Command and General Staff College. They worked in the Pentagon Building in staff assignments. I certainly do want to acknowledge the courage and bravery displayed by so many female personnel when under fire.

Due to our high school ROTC training and my summer training with the Citizens Military Training Corps, my buddy Francis Peter and I decided to enlist in the U.S. Army for fear that the war would be over before we could serve our country. Being commissioned was likely but not in the near term.

Like most young men during the Second World War, we promptly adapted to the rigors and discipline of Army life. Training developed in us a very high level of *esprit de corps*. We quickly learned the capabilities of our rifle, and other military equipment and vehicles, and also explosive techniques. Today, as a retired and as an "old soldier," I look back on my initial combat experience as a 2nd lieutenant and reflect on some questions such as:

- Did I execute my military duty faithfully? Yes

- Did the fear of injury or death stop me from my duty? Never

- Was I ever scared at certain times in combat? Of course

- In retrospect, with greater experience, could I have done more? Yes

- Did I acquire a love and respect for the United States Army? Totally

- Am I proud of the United States Army of today? Army commitment and courage is an example to all.

A lot of children of military families know very little about what their parent or family members did while preserving their freedom as well as the freedom of the nation. They only knew that their relative was "in the Army" or "in the service," and that they were away from home a lot. My hope is that this book may give my children (and their children and their children) a glimpse as to what their dad did in his youth and many Army years.

Lastly, I hope that anyone who reads this work will understand that I was no "Rambo," nor did I ever try to be a "shoot 'em up" guy. Yes, with my platoon we were at times committed to the fight as infantry. As such we suffered men wounded and killed. When not committed to our infantry mission, we always had the highest respect for our infantry brothers and did everything we could to alleviate their suffering and loss through our engineer and pioneer work. We also lost people in doing our work in minefields and removing booby traps.

My Early Military History

Some very special military dates are firmly etched in my memory. Other information was obtained or confirmed from the history of the 107th Engineers, the peacetime parent organization of the WWII 254th Engineer Combat Battalion. I was assigned to the 254th as a second lieutenant, platoon leader. Their previously-classified secret after-action report is now declassified. It identifies our deployment in our infantry combat operations in somewhat concise and brief military prose.

The day-to-day engineer/pioneer operations at the junior officer engineer cutting edge are still very vivid in my memory. While in the combat support engineer mode, just to the immediate rear of the line of enemy contact, we routinely performed these listed missions:

- Constructed bridges on floating pneumatic pontoons

- Built fixed timber trestle bridges

- Assembled portable steel panel bridges

(These bridges were capable of supporting continuous tank loads.)

- Demolition execution to impede or stop enemy force advance

- Installation of anti tank minefields

- Removal of enemy-installed minefields and roadblocks

- Constructed or improved roads/trails to facilitate ammunition, supply, evacuation of wounded and receipt of infantry replacements

- Destruction of enemy fortifications

- When time permitted preparation of gun emplacements

- Operated safe drinking water production at supply points

When the commanding general needed more infantry than was available on critical combat missions, the 254th Engineer Combat Battalion was reorganized as an infantry battalion. We parked our bulldozers, construction cranes, dump trucks, truck-mounted air compressors, demolition and pioneer equipment, construction tools and ceased quarry operations. We would go into combat with a strength of some 600-650 officers and men. The length of time could vary from a few days to a month.

As previously mentioned, my buddy, Francis Peter and I were very naive and concerned that the war could be over before we would be called up and might miss "the action." We therefore decided to enlist in the Army Corps of Engineers. We said goodbye to our families and friends and went to the local recruiting station to sign up. There were many other young men in line ahead of us. By the time we got to the head of the line the recruiting sergeant told everybody to return the next day since we had not yet been given our physical exams and taken the oath of allegiance. Discouraged, home we went as civilians to sleep again in our own beds, not the bunk beds in the barracks!

The next day, on 3 October 1942, we were first in line. We executed many forms, received our physical exams, were sworn in, and then told to join a long line of men that led to a tent about a city block distance away. The tent was located in an open field where we were to receive our immunizations.

Just as we were about to enter the medical tent, each person was given four or five different colored cards. The blue card for example would be for tetanus, a brown card for typhoid fever and so on. Medics were stationed at either side of the line at different locations inside the tent. As the recruit in front of me approached a station, that medic took the blue card and then gave him his tetanus shot. Another medic on the other side of the line gave the same recruit a shot in exchange for his brown card in the other arm. You received various shots until you had no more cards.

We were dressed only in our shorts. The person in front of me was a huge guy possibly 260 pounds. He said to me, "They can take one quart of my blood (donation) from each arm and two more quarts from my legs. I can't wait to go and shoot the enemy." I was completely in awe of this self-styled one-man army to be directly in front of me. But guess what? As the first medic approached him with the syringe, just before the needle could make contact with his arm, this guy fainted! So much for the one-man army. I never saw him again. Pete and I took our basic training at Ft. Belvoir, Virginia. Pete's Army serial number was 13105797. Mine was 13105800. We wore those numbers on our Identification Tags ("Dog Tags") throughout our enlisted service. As an officer, I was assigned a new commissioned officer serial number. Many years later, Social Security numbers were adopted for all ranks and branches of the military.

Until I enlisted in the Army (including my college days) I had always lived in my parents' home. Since being away from that environment for the first time in the Army, all of the military events described herein are permanently engraved in my memory. Throughout my career, I never maintained a diary or log or took notes.

Getting Started

Pete and I certainly learned a great many military techniques at Ft. Belvoir in basic training, and a significant number of social things. Among them for me was this interesting incident. During WWII most homes in the eastern part of the nation, and all troops barracks were heated with coal. Near the end of my basic training, I well remember an older (early thirties) soldier in my unit asking me to meet him behind the barracks coal pile. There he asked me to read to him a letter from his wife. Both of them were from the deep South. He mentioned that his wife also could not read nor write. After reading her letter, I then wrote a reply for him. Thank God that our country has come a very long way in education since those times.

At the completion of our basic training, Pete was selected to be a student taking a concentrated military map drafting course in Kentucky. When completed he was assigned to the 668th Engineer Topographic Company. Not long after joining his unit, it was scheduled for overseas movement. The good news was that well prior to that, he had talked with my dad and had obtained his blessing to propose marriage to my sister. Anne was now all grown up and a very pretty young lady. She accepted and they agreed to marry when Pete returned after the war. But more about that later.

My basic training company commander and an officer leadership committee interviewed me at the completion of my basic training. They questioned me about my student body school activities, Boy Scout participation, junior reserve officers training (ROTC) experience, Citizens Militia Training Corps (CMTC) knowledge, college pursuit of engineering, and my engineer field survey experience. Fortunately I was selected to attend the Engineer Officer Candidate School (OCS) also at Ft. Belvoir. I was subsequently commissioned a Second Lieutenant, U.S. Army Corps of Engineers on April 14th 1943. My initial commissioned assignment was with the 654th Engineer Topographic Battalion at Camp McCoy, Wisconsin. A very safe wartime map-making assignment.

Due to the urgent need for junior engineer officers recently commissioned to join overseas combat units which had no lieutenants, I, with other second lieutenants, were assigned to a replacement pool in October 1943, and ordered to report to the New York Port of Embarkation. I am still able to recall the names of the eleven other junior lieutenants whom I served with overseas. None of us knew each other prior to this time. Their names were: Arlan Bond, Norman Watkins, Allison Ware, Jack Davis, Mike Cosella, Reginald Fairfax, John Hix, Dominick Rubio, Warren Pomerantz, Adeloph Silberman, and Edwin Shaffer (and myself for those counting).

Off to War

We departed New York Harbor at night on the Queen Elizabeth en route to Europe. No convoy, no naval protection, no escort of any kind! She only had one five-inch gun on the stern, along with a Navy gun crew. Our then-classified ocean convoy number designation was RU870. Many abandon ship drills were conducted with each person wearing a life jacket. Many ships were torpedoed while crossing the oceans. On my voyage, a total of some 15,000 U.S. troops were aboard the "Queen," including 100 Army nurses. We never saw the nurses. They had armed Military Police (MPs) as guards. Their area was strictly "off limits" to all male military personnel. The ocean crossing only took three days. Each person was issued a colored card designating his eating times. He dared not lose that card!

An Unforgettable Shipboard Experience

Our replacement group of twelve Engineer second lieutenants were destined to be assigned to various engineer combat battalions in Europe that were under strength in junior officers. We were all quartered in a tiny stateroom that in peace time was one of the least expensive accommodations. We had tiered bunks along three walls. Field packs, carbines, life jackets, helmets, and other equipment were neatly stacked in the center of the so-called stateroom. There was one bathroom consisting of a shower (using seawater), toilet, wash sink and another strange-looking "toilet unit" that none of us had ever seen before. Later we discovered that it was not a toilet!

After several days at sea, one of the guys was sitting on the regular toilet. At the very same time my buddy Second Lieutenant Jack Davis had the trots real bad. He sat on the adjacent "toilet" and later when he pulled the chain to flush, we all quickly determined that it definitely was not a regular toilet. Eleven other guys were not happy, but we all liked Jack.

When the "Queen" arrived, she docked at Gorick, Scotland, again at night. We were quickly offloaded and we then boarded a blacked-out troop train which took us to a replacement depot. The "Queen" promptly departed again for the USA to continue bringing more troops to England for the eventual invasion of France.

All of us were assigned to the 254th Engineer Combat Battalion, stationed in the ocean vacation (during peacetime) village of Newquay in Cornwall, England (near Land's End). It will sound strange, but it was somewhat like Carmel-by-the-Sea in California. But the sandy beach at Newquay had been heavily mined by the British in anticipation of a German invasion attempt earlier in the war. On arrival the Battalion Commander, Lt. Col. Loren Jenkins called us into a room and announced that he had previously recruited most of the personnel when the unit was in National Guard status. He personally knew and had trained most of the senior non-commissioned officers (NCOs), and that he would have preferred to commission them if he could in lieu of receiving a batch of new 2nd lieutenants that he did not know. He also said that there would be no promotions until we had proved ourselves on the Continent in combat.

That was not the "welcome" orientation we had expected since all of us had a strong desire to excel. Presumably, he wanted to set a very sober tone, and he sure did. His senior NCOs were aware of his feelings. Nevertheless, things worked out okay. The battalion was billeted in several blocks of requisitioned British row houses. I was assigned to Company B as a platoon leader of 43 men. The platoon sergeant directly under me was an old National Guard soldier whose name was Maurice Syrjala. The overall mission of Army Combat Engineers was, by employing engineer skills, to facilitate the advance of Allied combat forces, and stop or delay the enemy. Also, to assume the infantry role when required by the tactical situation.

Preparing for Combat

During WWII, many combat engineers were ordered to England to construct camps and training areas to accommodate the infantry, airborne, armored divisions, and logistic troops that were scheduled to arrive later from the United States.

The Army also recognized the need for a training invasion beach complex complete with concrete pillboxes barbed wire entanglements, booby traps, mines, "enemy" machine gun emplacement, beach and underwater obstacles of all types. The purpose was to expose, train, and condition the initial assault troops for their eventful operational commitment.

My battalion was assigned the mission of constructing and maintaining this "Training" invasion beach at a place identified as the Assault Training Center at Slapton Sands on the west coast of England. During those training exercises the 1st and 29th Infantry Divisions and attached units would load aboard Landing Ship Tanks (LSTs), Landing Craft Infantry (LCIs), Landing Craft Medium (LCMs), and Landing Craft Vehicle-Personnel (LCVPs) and be taken out to sea from secure areas. Troops were issued live ammunition and were out of sight from land. On command, the troops would assault the beach. At the same time, U.S. Army Air Corps P-47 fighter aircraft and Royal Air Force Spitfires (RAF) would bomb and strafe the beach with live ammunition. Artillery units afloat also fired at suspected beach targets. It was very realistic training.

Specialized Demolition Training

At the completion of the Assault Training Center Beach Construction Project, the battalion began preparing for their invasion training by going out to sea, then over the side of an LST, going down rope ladders, and dropping into a bobbling little LCVPs. Then run for the beach five miles away. However, at the same time the battalion commander was ordered to send two officers for training by British Commandos in specialized demolition operations at the Royal Engineer School in Ripon, Yorkshire, England. Lt. Jack Davis and I were selected.

At that time the British Commandos were much more experienced in all types of explosive detection, removals, and demolition neutralization than the U.S. Army. This was due to their unfortunate combat experience in the Dieppe Raid, and the British evacuation of their forces at Dunkirk and Singapore. Due to this special training selection, Jack and I missed going out to sea with our battalion, and descending the rope ladders into those bobbing LCVPs.

Jack Davis was my buddy. He was the big guy and I was not as tall as Jack. He was from Corbon, Kentucky. Single, six-foot-four, some 230 pounds, and handsome. The only negative thing about Jack was his drinking. He was popular with the other junior officers, his men, and the ladies. I did not drink or smoke and did not go to the local English pubs (bars), but Jack did.

We were very close. Jack would do just about anything for me, and I for him. On more than one occasion, someone would tell me to hurry to a pub and drag Jack out of there before the MPs or local police would get him. I would go in and hit him in the arm as hard as I could. He would turn around to slug the person who had hit him. On seeing me, he would say something like, "Buddy, don't hit me." I would take him by the hand and get him back to our quarters. He used to kid me by saying that he had never worn shoes until he entered the Army. It would crack me up, of course, because I knew better. More about Jack later.

Since we were Americans, Jack and I were required to eat in the British Brigadier General Officers mess. The food ration was somewhat limited in relation to what was served in the U.S. Army. In order to get a more ample portion of food, I arranged a movie date with a British enlisted woman who served the food as the waitress at our table. At that time, it was strictly forbidden for any male officer to date an enlisted woman.

I had no personal interest in the young lady. My only goal was to get a little more generous portion of food. Sometimes she would put an extra small portion of meat under the potatoes. The night of the so-called date, the British MPs saw us. They took extra delight in catching an American officer since we were better paid and had more money to spend. British women also thought the US uniforms were more attractive than the British. Anyhow, they blew their whistles and shouted, "Stop Yank!" I told her to run in one direction while I ran the other way. The MP's did not go after her. They wanted the Yank! I climbed over fences (in total wartime black out), through gates, yards and the like without being caught. That was the first and last time I ever did that.

After graduation from the Special British Demolition School, Lt. Davis and I returned to our unit in Newquay just in time to participate in manual construction of portable steel bridges. The Battalion

Commanding Officer (CO) would have the non-commissioned officers and officers compete against each other at adjacent bridge sites to determine which group was the fastest in construction time. The enlisted soldiers were permitted to watch the competition and generally cheer the NCOs. It was much fun and excellent training. Both groups quickly became experts. In actual operations, of course, the enlisted soldiers performed the manual labor tasks with NCOs running special crews while the officers did the design work, logistics, selection, and overall direction.

Waste Not, Want Not

To preclude U.S. troops from consuming scarce British rations, the Army had all troops' food sent to England via convoys from the U.S.A. A significant number of those ships were sunk by German submarines. U.S. Army Lt. General John C. H. Lee was responsible for the safe receipt and proper consumption of all supplies. One of his pet projects was the elimination of waste. One day he arrived at our battalion at noon time unannounced. He went directly to a mess hall to see what items were going into the garbage cans. He observed a soldier throwing a small unused slice of bread into the waste container. At that point he had the soldier stand by the container while he sent for the battalion commander, company commander, and all company officers. After a stern lecture on the cost of waste in maritime lives, ships, fuel, and food, he ended the scene by eating that slice of bread!

At every meal thereafter, as long as we were in England, a screen was placed over the garbage can while an officer (by roster selection) was stationed there. The only items permitted for disposal were bones, coffee grounds, and egg shells. He sure made his point. Not only that company, but all companies. And yes, I also had to take my turn on "garbage watch."

"Fire in the Hole"

Immediately after the bridge training, the Corps Commanding General (three stars) ordered our CO to have one engineer lieutenant and four enlisted demolition specialists develop a basic demolition training program. The training would be designed to include practical exercises for non- engineer troops in recognition and avoidance of enemy-implanted explosives. I was selected. Meanwhile, the rest of the Battalion departed to train with our Navy in amphibious beach landing operations.

I will never forget one of the artillery battalions I trained. The battalion commander asked me if the many antitank mines he carried could be buried in a large hole/trench at a narrow road passage through which the German armored vehicles would have to pass to attack his artillery guns, equipment, and men.

My answer was in the positive. I showed the entire battalion of about 600 men how to calculate the desired amount of TNT required. Each anti-tank mine contained five pounds of TNT. Then I demonstrated how to detonate the explosives using time fuses and the electric firing method. We also showed them how to compute the safe distance to be away from the explosion.

We had six holes dug; loaded plastic explosive in the fuse well of one land mine per hole. I stressed that the fused mine must be in direct physical contact with the other mines.

Two officers and three NCOs were then selected to prepare the fuses and complete the installation for demolition. I primed the first hole. With the battalion about three city blocks away in distance, I began ordering the explosion in sequence with the order, "Fire in the hole." Everything went well until charge #6. The NCO who prepared that hole lit his time fuse. We waited for it to explode but nothing happened. After a misfire, training regulations require that 30 minutes time must pass before the misfire can be investigated. Not so in combat of course.

I was using a public address system. On it I asked, "Who is going to go down there and take that charge apart?" Looking around, I noticed that a lot of soldiers were looking at the ground, the sky their uniforms...anywhere but at me. Nobody said a word. I announced that since I was the instructor, I was responsible and I would have to do it. I wanted to take the NCO who screwed up with me. But I did not. As I was about twenty feet away from the buried explosive charge, a huge fire ball and thick black smoke engulfed me. I could feel the intense heat and see steel antitank mine cases on fire falling all around me. Was I surprised? Hell yes. Injured? No.

The troops being trained were sure that I was in little pieces. The charge did not detonate. It did, however, deflagrate. The primed mine exploded, but it was not in physical contact with the adjacent mines. TNT will burn like wood. When that mine case exploded, it then ruptured the nearby steel mine cases causing their TNT to deflagrate underground instead of detonate. With sufficient oxygen, heat, and pressure it finally erupted! I had almost had it.

However, when that total mission was completed, my soldiers and I returned to our battalion just in time to repack our equipment for the D-Day Invasion operation, code-named "Overlord."

As mentioned before, my engineer battalion had the benefit of loading the landing ship tanks (LSTs), going out to sea, shipboard training, going over the side and down the large rope ladders and into the small landing craft vehicle personnel (LCVPs). The LCVPs have a ramp in the front that are lowered when the craft is on a beach or near the shore. The problem is that the heavier LST rides more steady in the water where the tiny LCVPs are bobbing up and down and banging against the LST. If you don't judge correctly a soldier can be crushed between the LST and the LCVP. Or get dumped into the ocean with 70-80 pounds of gear on his back.

As I said, the specially trained demolition soldiers in my platoon and I were away on detached service training non-engineer troops so we missed the invasion training. We would do it "for real" the first time in the initial landing operations.

D-Day Invasion Planning

Once locked in our battalion staging area, we were told to anticipate the D-Day landings where German engineers would have demolished four critical bridges in a marshy region beyond the beachhead. One of those bridges was assigned to my platoon for repair. (That bridge is marked on an original map issued to us before the landing.)

If destroyed, our army could not bring needed replacement soldiers and ammunition forward, nor evacuate wounded for transfer to England. One of those bridges was pre-assigned to me which later became a problem involving a Brigadier General, my air compressor operator, and me, which I will address later.

When the battalion reached the D-Day assigned staging tent area in England we found that we were inside a barbed wire quadrangle area with four elevated machine gun towers manned by U.S. soldiers at each corner. We were told that should anyone attempt to leave through the barbed wire fence, U.S. guards in those towers had been instructed to shoot to kill. We could not talk to our tower guards, much like being prisoners of an enemy. There must have been hundreds of similar isolated camps elsewhere n England.

Our "containment" area was near a seaport town called Falmouth in Southwest England. We were told that we then were completely sealed in and segregated from the rest of the world.

Once inside, we were issued maps of the Normandy, France D-Day Invasion Beaches, invasion currency, two blankets, live ammunition, and anti-seasick pills, ration food bars for three days, the password and reply (for three days), wool uniform and wool underwear treated against potential enemy chemical agents, inflatable life belt, and many, many other items.

A completely new item for troops that was issued to all personnel in my battalion was a very small self injection type morphine syrette tube, to be used only should one suffer a life-threatening wound. The morphine would be used if the soldier was isolated, mortally wounded, and without the possibility of receiving medical help. This item was only issued after being in "lock-down."

The morphine was taped to the inside of our helmet liner neck strap. The syrettes were all collected within four or five days after the landing and we never saw them again. I presume the same confiscation was implemented for all other initial combat troops.

In the battalion tent staging area, there was a top secret detailed terrain scale model of each of the landing areas. From tiered wooden bleachers we would study the model so that with our eyes closed we knew where to land, the exit trails, cottage locations, distant church steeples and the like. We could picture exiting from our landing crafts to Omaha Dog Red Beach.

There was no doubt where we were going now! Total initial allied fighting strength for D-Day was some 175,000 men. Our engineer combat battalion of some 650 men was a very small portion of the 100,000 men of the First U.S. Army, commanded by General Omar

Bradley. Another 75,000 men came from England, Canada, and smaller contingents from Poland, Czechoslovakia and the Netherlands.

Having been away from my unit for much of the time, I hardly knew the names of the 43 men in my platoon. Without prior warning, I received three extra soldiers. When I asked why, I was told that they were replacements in anticipation of men I might lose. Not a happy thought.

The entire battalion was told that it was a component of landing force "B." We had no idea as to the composition of other landing force "B" units, or their missions. It was assumed that Landing Force "A" would be ahead of us and that we would be supporting them. The mission of the Corp V was universally understood. The two V corps assault infantry divisions were the 1st Infantry Division (known as the Big Red One) and the 29th Infantry Division and special troops attached non-divisional organizations like Artillery, Armor, and Combat Engineers.

Days before boarding the LST on the morning of June 5th, instructions were issued that all officers would have a vertical three-inch white stripe, one inch wide stenciled on the center rear of the helmet. NCOs had the same stripe size only stenciled horizontally. This was done so that troops to the rear could promptly recognize their combat leaders. I did not think that this was such a good idea since it would make us prime targets for the enemy snipers, but I complied.

We loaded onto LST 484. Prior to that, many of our guys had their hair cut in a Mohawk style and sharpened their bayonets. As mentioned previously, the classified D-Day code name for the total invasion was "Overlord." The invasion had been delayed due to storms and later high seas. As the world soon learned, the invasion of Europe was June 6, 1944 at dawn (6:00am). Hitler preferred to refer to the European continent as his "Festung Europa" (Fortress Europe).

Aboard Ship

U.S. Navy Lt. O'Rourke, the equivalent of an army captain, was the LST skipper. He had us bed down on the steel deck together with our CO. The rest of the ship was loaded with all kinds of combat vehicles, which would be off loaded after combat troops had control of the immediate beach area. The Army had pre-positioned "C"-rations on board the LST for our food. These were in a little container about the size of a Cracker Jack box. The little food container had a four-ounce tin can of eggs or meat, hard crackers, a stick of chewing gum, four cigarettes, a small candy bar, and a little toilet paper. When Lt. O'Rourke saw that, he said, "On my ship, everybody eats Navy chow." Instead of the "C"-rations, all troops enjoyed good Navy food.

In our short time onboard, we saw that the lowest rank sailor had a nice clean bunk with a little reading light, always great food, and a washing machine at his disposal. We soldiers washed, shaved, and washed our socks and underwear in our steel helmets.

The skipper told us that Army officers could use the bunks of his officers when they were on watch. The naval officers' ward room (dining room) had been modified where dining tables would be operating tables with large medical room lights suspended from above.

Going to War

Up to this point, our ship was relatively safe in British-controlled waters. However, early on the morning of June Fifth, we set off for the beaches of France on the other side of the British Channel. We were well-briefed on our initial missions.

As part of a large ship force, our battalion was awaiting our landing force "B" orders, when unexpectedly a small but very swift craft with a powerful public address system approached our LST. A question was bellowed out, "Are there any engineers aboard?"

Our battalion commander, Lt. Colonel Jenkins, answered, "Affirmative."

Then the call from the swift craft was, "Send an engineer platoon ashore immediately."

The CO replied that we have prior specific missions assignments and then asked, "By whose authority?"

The quick reply was, "By order of the Beach Commander."

Colonel Jenkins then turned to Captain Minor and said. "Your company's mission. Who will you send?"

Minor replied, "Ramos and his platoon since they have the most experience." Minor then said, "Ramos, it's your assignment." The little swift craft official said we would be removing barbed wire, anti-personnel mines, demolishing fortifications and mine clearing and to bring TNT blasting caps, detonating cord, blasting machines, mine detectors, and bayonets for probing. With all that equipment it was thought that we might not be able to carry our weapons. I assembled my platoon, issued instructions, ordered that WE WOULD carry our weapons and ammo. I was sure that the guy in that little power boat had not been on the beach. I was a "green" 2nd lieutenant (like everyone else) in my first command. But not that green. Anyway, there went the bridge construction or repair mission that we planned for while in England.

Since our battalion was part of Landing Force "B," I felt sure that the infantry was identified as LF "A."

The little landing crafts were designed to deliver forty or so soldiers or a single large truck, a jeep with trailer, or similar vehicles to a beach. The bow could be lowered to become a discharge ramp. Great concept. The realities of war were greatly different. The LST (mother ship) rode 20/30 feet above the 'baby' LCVP. Wave action would force or slam the little LCVP's against the side of the much longer vessel.

I checked my men, their equipment, explained our mission with the very limited information available, and my platoon and I went over the side and down rope ladders and into a LCVP with all of the combat equipment that we could carry. The water was very choppy and we had lots of equipment on our backs. The other half of that exercise was to get into a little bobbing LCVP. Depending on wave action, at times it would slam against and then fall away from the hull of the larger LST. It was a very sobering first-time experience. Only one of many more to come.

Large diameter rope ladders were thrown over the ship rails, extending down the side just above the water surface. This made it possible for troops to descend into the smaller boats. With high seas and waves slamming the little crafts against the LST, I later learned that some unfortunate soldiers were crushed first as they were about to drop into their landing craft. Others let go of the rope ladder just as the LCVP was sucked away from the LST. These poor guys drowned due to the excessive weight we all carried. All of my guys made it to shore okay.

Many men became casualties, and not only by enemy bullets or artillery. Our ship to ship descent experience was obtained in the actual combat environment. All that time, my pre-planning bridge mission assigned while in England was no longer likely. Accordingly, my soldiers and I were the first members of our combat engineer battalion to be off loaded from LST 484 into little LCVPs and into the beach. It was quite a sobering experience for me since I was responsible for this new mission, and for the safety and lives of 46 men, a few who were close to the age of my father. Others my age. This newly-assigned mission was, of course, foremost on my mind.

Once all aboard the LCVP we headed towards Omaha Dog-Red Beach. On the way in, the LCVP operator said that he was not Navy but a U.S. Coast Guardsman (USCG). I told him that he should be guarding the Mississippi or Potomac Rivers, not here. He said, "That's why I joined the Coast Guard!" A short time thereafter our LCVP was damaged as we neared the beach, possibly from an underwater spike, debris, or other anti-boat device. The USCG operator said that he could no longer control the craft and he lowered the bow ramp saying "Everybody out!"

We then went out, into the water. I'm sure that the water was above my head; and with our extra gear, I truly don't remember how I made it ashore. Maybe I swam or more like I "walked on the water." I truly don't know. More likely the adrenaline kicked in and somehow I got ashore. Everybody got ashore okay with all of our weapons and demolition equipment. A lot of other guys who had been hit while in the water likely squeezed their life belts to inflate them. However, since the belt was worn low around the waist, if you lost consciousness (loss of blood, shock wound) your body reacted like the inverted letter "U," with the head and feet below water and the waist on the water surface. If you were not already dead, you drowned.

The Allied navies had shelled beaches and the various air fleets had bombed and strafed the area as well. The invasion beach looked like the thousands of craters on the moon, and just as desolate. Due to the massive U.S. Army Air Corps bombing campaign (the Army Air Corps was the precursor to the U.S. Air Force). The naval shelling certainly caused the death of exposed German soldiers from concussion or shell fragments. Nevertheless, great numbers of enemy were not injured and were full of fight. It was like poking a stick in a nest of yellow jackets. Thank God we were hours behind those very first guys.

Aside from the steel anti-boat obstacles that the enemy placed below the water line, with anti-tank German Teller Mines facing seaward. Above the water line, the Germans also anchored telephone poles pointing seaward. These poles were fitted with antitank steel mines containing 12 pounds of cast TNT facing us. There were also pointed steel spikes inclined to seaward, railroad rails, barbed wire and other obstacles to destroy landing craft and impede allied foot troops.

When on Omaha Dog-Red Beach, I noticed U.S. dead guys with these special three-inch white stripes helmet markings. Additionally, many of the dead were combat junior leaders, officers, and NCOs who were armed with carbines. Much different in appearance from the standard infantry Garand rifle M-1. Personnel armed with the .45 caliber pistol or the Browning Automatic Rifle (BAR) also received, in my mind, special enemy attention. I quickly took some grease from a knocked out Jeep and covered that white stripe on the rear of my helmet and my little lieutenant's gold bar on the front. I also ditched my carbine and grabbed an M-1 Garand rifle and carried it all through the war. I was learning fast.

On the beach there were signs containing the German words "Achtung Minen" (Attention Mines) with the skull and crossbones painted thereon. Narrow paths outlined with guiding barbed wire suggested a so-called safe path through the minefields. You never knew if those "safe paths" were really zeroed in with enemy mortars, machine gun, or artillery fire as killing zones. Going into a marked mine field was also a very sobering thought. That was not an option for me! And then there were the fortified concrete pillboxes. Thank God our infantry had managed to get through those defenses well ahead of us and we were spared that event.

The beach was littered with dead bodies, destroyed military equipment, craters and all sizes of metal fragments everywhere. That made it practically impossible to use our mine detectors since they were designed to detect buried metallic mines and booby traps. With every sweep you received continuous erroneous ferrous metal mine alert signals. Therefore, we probed with bayonets and looked for visual signs as well.

We began clearing a path in the direction of the nearest village. When we saw an exposed mine or suspicious round depression of antitank configuration, we blew them up in place. During this time we came under direct rifle fire. It was difficult to pinpoint the source since large holes and craters were everywhere. When we received enemy fire, we would return the fire in the suspected general direction but not sure of its exact location. This delayed us in our mine-clearing mission. Later an Army ranger appeared and said if we would continue our mine demolition operation, he would take care of the rifle fire. I agreed and he departed.

Sometime later he reappeared with a German Army prisoner. I suspected that the prisoner had been drinking, which, thank God, negatively impacted his rifle accuracy. The sergeant told me this was the guy who has been shooting at us, and said he was now our prisoner. I replied that I did not have the resources to guard him and at the same time to continue my demolition mission. I said, "You captured him, he's your prisoner. Take care of him." He said okay and left with the prisoner.

Later that day I had to go towards the beach with some of my soldiers to locate more explosives. Along the path I noticed a dead German soldier. On inspection, I recognized him as the prisoner the sergeant was supposedly going to hand over to proper authorities for evacuation to England. I was sure that he had murdered that unarmed prisoner. During WWII, U.S. military personnel did not have their names taped or stenciled on their uniforms. I had no way of identifying the Ranger and I had to get back to my men with more explosives. If I could, I would have had him court-martialed. As time went on, I frequently thought about that day and I said to myself, possibly some other German soldier may have unknowingly evened up the score. Who knows? Over the years, I have always prayed for the repose of that prisoner's soul.

The sandy beach area revealed much destruction of life and equipment, especially just beyond the waters edge. One scene I will never forget. Shortly after coming ashore, I noticed a U.S. 29th Infantry

Division soldier that had no torso. Only boots and a pair of legs. Next to those remains was his Browning Automatic Rifle. On the wood rifle stock I saw the photo of a pretty young woman holding a beautiful little infant baby. To protect the picture, he had it covered with a heavy clear plastic. Of course that young woman did not know then that she was a widow, and her little baby would have no loving daddy. But I knew.

First Night Ashore

Since I was operating alone, as late evening was approaching, I began to plan as to where and how I'd provide security for my platoon of 46 soldiers that first night. We were not in contact with any friendly forces and I had no idea where our battalion would be located or if it was even ashore. Ahead of us was a small group of farmhouses adjacent to an old stone church. I was just about to break into the church for security, when a priest in a black cassock realized what I was about to do. I had one man in my platoon who spoke fluent French. His name was Malafont. The priest told him that the Germans would likely shell the church steeple since the Americans would certainly use them for observation purposes. He said that we would be safer in a friend's residence since he knew the family would safely help us until the next day.

Norman houses are constructed of stone walls about two feet thick. I elected to take his advice. I realized that he could be a German agent in the garb of a priest, but I took the chance. The home was occupied by a woman in her late 40's and her pretty young blonde daughter about twenty years of age.

The mother's husband was in another nearby village when the invasion began and German troops would not permit any civilian movement on roads or trails. We were told by the wife to go up into the attic for the night. There was only one ceiling entry/exit access. I was not pleased about that since in an emergency everyone would have to exit through that opening. I heard my men talking about the pretty blonde French girl. Realizing that we had been confined in England behind barbed wire, and afloat for a total of three weeks these guys had not even seen a female for quite some time. I then had a talk with my soldiers and said for them not to even think about her.

That night German troops reentered the little hamlet and actually occupied the very house we were in, as possibly some sort of head-quarters. We could hear them talking. Thank God they did not search the attic or throw a hand grenade up there in lieu of a search. We would all have been dead or at least prisoners of war. I still had a lot to learn. One of my guys, Lou Chimera, had been a professional baseball player with the New York Giants. Lou was a big guy, and he fell into a deep sleep and had a nightmare. We woke him quickly to avoid him giving us away to the enemy downstairs.

Later in the night, unknown to us, the Germans evacuated the area. We had no idea as to what was going on. Early the next morning, we heard American commands in English and we knew everything was okay to move out. As we were leaving the French girl's house, she came over to me and put a little white rosebud in the button hole of my shirt pocket. She said that we were the first Americans that she had ever seen, and that she would pray that I and my soldiers would survive the war and return to our homeland and families unharmed. That innocent little gesture caused all kinds of speculation in the minds of my virile soldiers. They were sure that "the Lieutenant" somehow had managed to see her alone. Wrong!

On the way back to locate our battalion area, an elderly French farm woman motioned to me to follow her to her house. When I arrived she showed me an interior wall that had been partially penetrated by an artillery shell. The fuse nose cone protruded about two to three inches into her room. She asked me to pull it out so that she could eventually resume residence after the fighting moved on. I was not about to touch that shell since it was then very super sensitive. I tried to explain that to her. She only wanted me to remove the shell. I finally said "au revoir" to her and departed with my guys.

Soon I saw an American soldier and asked him had he heard of any engineer units in the vicinity. He showed me on my map where he had seen some of them. Shortly thereafter we located our battalion.

When we finally joined the battalion and reported to my company C.O., we quickly began performing engineering work such as filling bomb craters, reinforcing bridges to accommodate the weight of expected friendly tanks, artillery, and other heavy vehicles. Sweeping road and shoulders with mine detectors to locate and remove buried mines was also a very high priority.

Sometimes the German Army Engineers would bury two antitank mines in the same hole. The first mine would be buried deeper with a dirt covered wire that was attached to its firing mechanism and to the "bait" top buried mine's firing mechanism. When the top "discovered" mine was moved or disturbed - one or both would explode. Nasty trick.

The Build-Up

As our infantry continued to advance in the "Hedgerow Country," the army increased the troop buildup in the rear to make possible a deep strategic penetration of enemy lines. We had never heard of French hedgerows nor trained for them, so the term needs an explanation.

Many hundreds of years ago when the initial French settlers begin clearing their land for agriculture, they recognized that the land was covered with rocks and boulders. To eliminate this problem they would build stone walls five to seven feet in height, with a foundation four to six feet thick. The walls would indicate overall property boundaries, and within those enclosures individual crop fields of the same farm. Where separate farms would meet, the continuous rock walls would continue uninterrupted for miles. To landscape and add character and strength, shrubs and vines were planted within the walls. The roots and vines over time acted as a reinforcing material to greatly strengthen the already thick walls. With many years of growth, they greatly increased in height and served as a high hedge. The original earth roads and trails evolved into sunken lanes that were now eight to ten feet below the top of the stone-hedge walls.

To attack the enemy, our infantry had to climb up and over these onerous obstacles. The German riflemen were positioned prone on top of the opposite wall, while their machine gunners would be firing through prepared ground level opening with devastating effect. Combat engineers blew exit holes with limited success. An improved tactic with accompanying automatic firepower was needed.

When our tanks tried to ram the walls they would not bulge. Finally an ordinance sergeant came up with an idea to weld several long steel shafts to the tanks front to act as a multi-faced plow. When tests were conducted, the results were a great success. Thereafter, the tanks would penetrate the stone walls, followed quickly by infantry who would fan out and attack the enemy. They would then have the direct support of their tanks, machine guns, and main cannon. Who knows how may lives were saved by this innovative technique. And the war went on without interruption.

Meanwhile, the large tank/armor forces of General George Patton's Third Army, which was in England during the initial Normandy landings, was now awaiting its opportunity and seaborne transportation to join the war in Normandy. In order to give Patton's tanks the maneuvering room to penetrate deep into enemy territory, General Bradley's predominantly infantry forces spread out, thinning our infantry front lines, and replacing them with engineer combat battalions. My battalion was one of such units. On July 19, 1944 we took over some of the 2nd Infantry Divisions's front line fox holes, machine gun positions, and outposts along a mile-wide front of the first battalion, 9th Infantry Regiment's defensive positions. This was our first reorganization in our role as an infantry battalion in combat. The official (then classified) battalion history reported that during the period of July 19th to 28th eight of our men were killed and 24 were wounded.

Hitler was concerned that Patton's tank army could be landed on the shorter Pas-de-Calais coast. Accordingly, large German tank forces were positioned midway between Normandy and Pas-de-Calais. My platoon occupied the extreme outer right edge of the battalion. Our tactical positions in a field were near a little hamlet called Berigny. There were no friendly troops on my immediate right. Only a void in the line of about a half-mile to our neighbor, the 9th Infantry Regiment of the 2nd Infantry Division. We ran probing combat patrols from my platoon to their infantry outposts and they did the same to us. All patrols operated at different times. The purpose was to determine enemy strength, their positions, their intentions, and to confuse the enemy and determine if German units knew that we were weak at those points. We also needed to know if such troops were getting into our rear. Our engineer machine gunners were always busy in our support.

As a platoon leader my job was to direct the operations of the entire platoon and, of course, not leave the bulk of my command to go with a few soldiers on a patrol. We fired our 30- and 50-caliber machine guns into the enemy positions, and they would return our fire. If my memory serves me correctly, we were opposed by the 6th Parachute Regiment of the 5th Parachute Division of the German Army.

One day I overheard one of my soldiers commenting to his buddy that he had made so many patrols and that the Lieutenant had not gone on a single patrol as yet. When I overheard that remark, I decided to take the next patrol myself. I knew that would put an end to such thoughts or comments. I told my platoon sergeant that I was going on the next patrol, and off I went with two other soldiers.

While I was on patrol, it just happened that Lt. Col. Jenkins the battalion commander had a mission that he wanted me to accomplish. We had sound power telephones to all elements down to and including the platoons. The only power requirement for these combat telephones was the human voice itself. Jenkins called my company commander, Captain Minor, and told him to have me report to him without delay. Minor called my platoon headquarters asking for me. When he was told that I was on patrol, he knew I was in trouble with the Old Man. When Jenkins was told that I was on patrol, he said, "If he gets back, have him report to me."

On my return, Captain Minor said the colonel wanted to see me now. When I reported to him, he proceeded to chew me out royally. Among other things, he said, "Ramos, if you want to act like a corporal I can arrange that." And on and on, and that was the nice part! He then went on to say, "That whenever the entire platoon was engaged in an operation you had better blankety-blank be leading it. I'm losing lieutenants fast enough. Do you understand, Lieutenant?"

He was gracious enough to let me have the last two words. "Yes, Sir!" Then he said, "You are also relieved of command." When I returned to the company, I told Captain Minor and he said he knew before I told him but as of midnight you are back in command. That was the first time, but not the last time that I was relieved of my command. It was a good lesson for me. Also important was that my men knew that I had gone out on a small combat patrol. I never did know just what the mission was that Colonel Jenkins wanted me to undertake that day.

Being Careful

During this combat operation, between our lines and the enemy positions there was a stream some four to six feet deep. On the other side of the stream, there was a square shaped farmhouse. It was so positioned that I could see two of its four sides at the same time, looking somewhat like the bow of a ship coming towards you. Lt. Jack Davis wanted to know what if anything was contained in that farmhouse. Also leaving his platoon, he took off to investigate. After he was beyond earshot, I saw a German paratrooper approaching from the other wall to the very same corner that Jack was headed for. Jack could not hear our warning. They both reached the corner at the very same moment. Helmets collided and both of them fell backwards to the ground. At the same time both soldiers began firing their weapons as each man fell to his rear. Neither man was hit! It was almost humorous to see the dust rise from their boots as they pushed against the dirt to get traction and get out of there. Jack was lucky since neither Capt. Minor nor Col. Jenkins knew of his reconnaissance.

To our direct front we could occasionally see in the distance the movement of enemy soldiers. That would cause us to bring our machine gun fire on those targets of opportunity, which, of course, resulted in their return fire on us. There was, however, one target that we did not immediately fire on. It was called the field latrine. It's a narrow trench the width of a shovel three to four feet deep with a vertically positioned stick in the ground supporting a roll of toilet paper, with a large tin can over the paper top to keep it dry. When the soldier straddled the trench to answer nature's call, we did not fire. However, the moment he had his pants up, he was fair game. You should have seen that guy move. I doubt that we ever got one that way due to the distances involved. For sure, we well camouflaged our latrines.

Some three to four hundred feet directly in front of our dug in positions was the remains of a 29th Infantry Division soldier. He had likely been shot several weeks earlier and with the hot summer temperatures of June 1944, the odor was overwhelming. Lt. Col. Jenkins told Captain Minor that a dead American soldier's body directly before our lines was bad for morale. Jenkins said, "Get that body out of here and deliver it to the quartermaster for identification and burial."

This order was received not long after my "two man patrol episode." Accordingly, Capt. Minor assigned the mission to me.

I selected four of my men telling them to sprinkle some talcum powder on cotton, placing the cotton inside our gas masks to reduce the stench. We also took an Army wool blanket to remove the remains. Since the enemy was on the opposite hill, we crawled to the body. We were not fired on; possibly because they also wanted to be rid of the smell. The decaying odor of thousands of U.S. and German troops, along with civilians and all kinds of animals was very pervasive.

On arrival we noticed that the white body had turned black or deep brown and that it was being consumed by maggots. We tried to pull him onto the blanket. That did not work since the skin cracked or separated and the maggots spewed out. We were finally able to roll him onto the blanket and pull the blanket back to our lines. On return, Capt. Minor had the remains loaded on a rear area truck for delivery to a temporary quartermaster burial site. That was the end of my involvement.

After combat moved further inland, specially trained quartermaster support troops went into the former combat areas to remove, identify, and organize temporary cemeteries for both friendly and enemy troops in different locations. Combat troops are not trained for this type of mission. Quartermaster soldiers collected the deceaseds' identification ("dog") tags, rings, pocketbooks, letters, pictures, and other items for identification and eventual delivery to the next of kin.

Another thing I well remember, as the German soldiers planned to withdraw or retreat or go to pre-planned fallback tactical positions, they would use forced civilian labor to prepare their subsequent combat bunker positions. They were lined with bed sheets overhead and on the walls. First they were used as trenches from which to fire at the advancing Allied troops. The sheets kept the dirt from falling on you and in your eyes when firing rifles or automatic weapons. It also facilitated night map reading and studying operational orders.

Their firing openings faced us, of course, since we were attacking them. When we occupied their captured positions their gun ports then faced to our rear. Accordingly, we dug our fox holes, since their tactical firing direction and gun ports were on the defense wall side and did not suit our tactical situation. Something else about the sheets. I noticed with them in place, a single candle provided a pretty good light. Many of their soldiers had fought in Russia and were much more experienced than us. But we were learning fast. Learning fast or you were dead.

Lt. Jack Davis - First Purple Heart

A few days after removing the dead infantry soldier in front of our combat positions, Jack Davis was injured in both hands from a white phosphorus grenade. He suffered a very serious burn injury that put him in the field hospital. After he was there for about a week, I had the opportunity to visit with him. As I entered the hospital tent ward full of combat wounded I saw him. Both hands were covered in bandages. He looked like he had white footballs for hands. A pretty young nurse, Lt. Frances Slanger, was giving him a sponge bath. As I approached his bed, Lt. Slanger had just about finished bathing him.

When he saw me coming he said to the nurse, "You have not washed me completely." She replied, "Lt. Davis, I have washed up as far as possible and I have washed down as far as possible." Then she put a lot of soapy water on the sponge, tossed it to Jack, and said "Lt. Davis, now you can wash possible." She then marched out of the tent ward amidst cheers, clapping, and good humor on the part of the other wounded patients.

The U.S. Air War

From our foxholes in the early morning we could see the U.S. Army Air Corps thousand-plane bombing formations en route to bomb Germany. A sight never to be forgotten. In the morning they would be flying at 12,000 to 15,000 feet above our foxhole positions. Unfortunately there would be fewer aircraft returning in the afternoon, and some of the damaged B-17 Flying Fortresses would be flying at 500 to 700 feet. Some had holes large enough to pass an automobile engine through them. Many had engines missing, but were still flying. Those guys certainly made our jobs less costly.

The Panzer Threat

Our army knew that a powerful German armored panzer division was being held in strategic reserve by Hitler since he had not known if the real invasion would come in the Pas-de-Calais area. That had been the most direct route from England to France, not the Normandy coast. The Normandy area was a much greater distance from England to France. The Panzer division was therefore stationed mid-way between the two potential invasion areas.

The Panzer division could only be committed to combat by a direct authorization from Hitler. The Panzers' mission was to drive the invasion force back into the sea. When it became clear that Normandy was the true invasion area, the Allied position was pitifully weak and we were barely holding on. As an example, our artillery guns were down to three rounds per gun, and they could only fire at a direct target. To make the American situation more grave, a storm over the Channel stopped all beach resupply operations. Our Army had to get along with what assets we had.

The situation was so critical that we could hear the Panzers in a few hedgerows in front of us. We were ordered to lay our antitank mines directly off our truck tailgates to the ground without any survey references or concealment. We were advised that if the weather was good the next morning that our P-38's, P-47's, and P-51's Fighter Aircraft would bomb and strafe the enemy armored forces.

First light of the next morning was a beautiful clear day, and here came those wonderful Army Air Corps fighters in great numbers. It reminded me of the movies where the settlers were attacked by Indians. The wagon master had circled the wagons. When the ammunition was almost all gone, and many of the men were wounded; it seemed as if there was no hope. But at the last moment, here came the cavalry and all was saved. Those fighter pilots reminded me of that classic movie situation.

When we later moved through the former German attack positions, we saw the massive destruction of Panzer tanks, artillery, infantry troop barriers, and enemy dead that had been inflicted by our planes.

After we were relieved of the infantry mission, we were more fully appreciative, on a very personal basis, of the valor and dedication of the infantry branch. We certainly had an enhanced respect for their critical role in the Army. They are rightfully called "The Queen of Battle." A reference to the queen on the chess board during our brief defensive period in the line, we had eight men killed and an additional twenty-four wounded for a total aggregate of thirty-two casualties. The longer in that role; the loss numbers would continue to increase.

Relieved of Command, Again

The war moved on and from my very narrow perspective of the situation, I thought that things were going along fairly well. Until one day when my platoon was repairing a bridge that German combat engineers had severely damaged as they were retreating. An unanticipated "visitor" changed my perspective.

Due to the intense summer heat, there had been a lot of head wounds suffered by American soldiers who were not wearing their helmets. For that reason the Army had wisely issued very specific orders for soldiers to wear their helmets at all times.

My men were working to reshape and repair a damaged bridge abutment. Compressed air for a jackhammer attachment was being supplied by the Le Roi air compressor. In the civilian world such hammers are used to break concrete, dense rock, and asphalt. At that time, before OSHA, equipment operators did not wear headgear. However, operating a jackhammer while wearing a steel helmet is just about impossible.

I had told the jackhammer operator several times to put his helmet back on. Finally, he said that the vibration caused the helmet to move forward hit his nose and repeatedly fall to the ground. In desperation he said "Lieutenant, if you want to get this bridge back in service, I can't work with this helmet on. It's helmet on and take forever; or helmet off and we return the bridge to operational service quickly." I said, "Mission first; no helmet."

A few minutes later, guess who is driving up in a jeep. A brigadier general (one star). The only general I personally saw during the entire war, by the way. He roared, "Who is in charge here?" I reported to him. He didn't seem to care about the bridge. His concern was that a soldier was not wearing his helmet. I tried to explain, but without success. He finally said, "Lieutenant, you are relieved of command. Notify your commanding officer."

When informed, the Old Man said, "For the rest of the day you can sensor mail." (An officer had to read all outgoing mail to ensure that no military information inadvertently would aid the enemy.) He then said, "Tomorrow you are back in command and back out there again!"

A Daring Reconnaissance

As previously mentioned, our battalion was one of many small units that was committed as an infantry battalion in the line along with other similar units, so as to give General Bradley (First Army Commander) the capability of concentrating large numbers of armored and infantry units at one critical location. This resulted in the Normandy Breakout. Thereby permitting General Patton's Third Army to use that opening for his deep penetration into France and the entrapment and surrender of thousands of German troops and destruction of their equipment.

At the completion of the Breakout, the 254th Engineer Combat Battalion was relieved of its infantry mission and returned to our primary engineer operations. At that time, Lt. Col. Jenkins sent for me, saying that a particular road containing a bridge that the enemy had been retreating over and likely had been damaged or destroyed. He wanted me to make a reconnaissance to determine its conditions, and come up with a bill of materials needed to restore the bridge to prompt service. He showed me on the map the bridge location and assured me that the bridge was now in U.S. hands.

My jeep driver's name was "Rebel." He and I took off for the bridge site. He was driving very slowly. Battle-wise soldiers knew to watch the ditches and road shoulders for communication telephone wire. The more wire, the safer was the area. As you went nearer the enemy, the less wire. When there was no wire, you knew that you were in the front line area. Since enemy patrols could "tap into" communication wires and monitor combat operations, there they used walkie-talkie radios.

As was customary in the combat area, windshields were flat on our jeep's hood to preclude the sun's reflection which signaled the enemy as to a target and also to facilitate prompt vehicle exit. I was checking the map and observing the wire. Finally there was no more wire and I saw soldiers dispersed in a large area crawling on their bellies with one man in the lead. Not a good sign.

Rebel was driving very slowly when the enemy began firing at our jeep. When we stopped there was a vacant one-man foxhole in the ditch adjacent to our jeep. Somehow Rebel and I both managed to occupy that same foxhole. I called to the lead soldier and asked him why he had not warned us. He said that he was the lead regimental scout to capture the bridge. Then he said, "If you wanted to be the lead scout, be my guest." Another close call.

With a lull in the firing, Rebel and I returned to our battalion and I reported first hand the conditions to Col. Jenkins. He said he'd inform higher headquarters. After that I always avoided Col. Jenkins.

Well after D-Day, about a month later, our chaplain was scheduled to visit and celebrate Holy Mass. The battalion was preparing to move into an infantry battalion's front line positions which was opposed by an experienced German army parachute battalion. I noted that prior to going into the line of contact, Mass attendance was very high. Once out of the line a few weeks later, and no longer in a daily high risk environment, the perceived need for God's protection was possibly minimized. I NEVER had that attitude.

Some weeks later I had to report to the Corps Engineer Staff Section in the rear area for special instructions. At the advance security checkpoint, I was stopped by the military police (MPs) and asked to present my War Department ID card. To my surprise I discovered that I had lost it; that wasn't something I needed to show near the front. The MPs then called one of the staff engineer people whom I knew, and he came to the checkpoint to identify me and confirm my unit.

About a month later I was called to my battalion headquarters where the battalion intelligence officer (S-2) returned to me my lost ID card. It seemed that after the battle for the bridge, the area was finally in US Army hands, another US soldier had used "my" foxhole. There he discovered the ID card. It went through intelligence channels to determine if I was deceased, and if not, in a hospital, or to what unit I was assigned. The ID card is a very important document should you be injured, taken prisoner, wounded, killed, or visiting a higher headquarters. I still have that first little ID card issued to me in about 1943.

About this time, my parents ,with my sister Anne, moved to 306 Normandy Drive in Silver Spring, a Maryland suburb of Washington.

On to Paris...with the Free French Army

The next big event for my battalion was being attached to the 2nd French Armored Division, a major combat unit commanded by French Army General Jacques LeClare, on its way to liberate Paris. For political reasons French General Charles de Gaulle asked U.S. General Eisenhower to include the assignment of French troops for participation in the liberation of the French capital. Eisenhower concurred; however; he attached U.S. combat elements to insure that once Paris was free, that the French combat troops would continue attacking the Germans beyond Paris, and to continue in our drive into Germany. For obvious political reasons, De Gaulle wanted to have French troops for a victory parade for him to review.

As Allied forces approached Paris, the German general who had been the German Military Governor of Paris for four years was ordered by Hitler to destroy all the beautiful bridges over the Seine River, along with the Eiffel Tower, the Louvre, Notre Dame Cathedral, statues, and all other art treasures in the city. Having lived in Paris during the German occupation, the German General loved the city and refused to execute the order.

Since there was no heavy organized fighting in Paris, the French soldiers (in U.S. tanks) said, "Cherchez la femme."For them their war was over, at least for a little while. I saw their tanks empty. No security! Many of the French soldiers I saw were from the French African colonies. Black men wearing red fez headgear and many of them had scars on each cheekbone. Some sort of manhood initiation. Our battalion arrived in Paris the 25th of August and moved out with other U.S. combat troops for further missions a few days later. We never knew when (or if) the French continued the German pursuit.

The largely untrained civilian French Forces of the Interior (FFI) underground elements warmly greeted us. When we appeared on the scene they quickly displayed their FFI arm bands. They all wanted to be acknowledged by their countrymen as heroes. They shot at anything and anybody. We kept well away from them.

While we were in Paris, the citizens were in ecstasy. They offered us wine, champagne, music, and dancing in the streets. By comparison the population in Normandy wore wooden shoes and old farm clothes. However, the people in Paris, especially the women, were very much more aware of their appearance and dressed better than the English or rural French women. Like all 22-year-old, young, single soldiers, we all were open to meeting a pretty young blonde French girl who spoke English.

On our first day, a young lady came up to me and said with a very strong French accent, "I speak English. I speak English."

I said, "Wonderful."

Then she said, "Do you like fruit?"

I said, "I love fruit."

She replied, "Bite my ass…it's a peach." Then she ran to another soldier repeating the same question. And then to another guy. And so on. Of course, we all said, "You speak very well." She had no idea what she was saying. Obviously, one of our guys with a sense of humor had taught her a phrase to deliver to the other American forces.

Having said goodbye to Paris on the 27th of August, troop payday was only four days away. By that time we were some miles from the city, and the Paris U.S. Army Finance Office. Each of our five companies had to send its own officer – I was one – to get the money for soldier payment (minus U.S. automatic allotments) in French francs. Arriving in Paris in late afternoon and after counting and signing for individual payrolls, I was anxious to get back to our units before dark. All five officers had barracks bags full of money. One of the officers said, "Before returning, let's take a break and we all visit a 'sporting house'."

One guy said, "There is a pretty lady. Maybe she can help us." When questioned she said, "I am very correct, but my girlfriend is in the business and I'll guide you there." At the "ladies of the evening's residence," I said that I would stay and guard the money. The other four guys said that was a good idea, since somebody has to guard the money. Later when they all returned smiling and in very good humor they said to me, "Buddy, now it's your turn." I replied that it was getting dark and some German combat patrols might erect roadblocks, string piano wire at neck height, and in darkness lay mines across the road. We better play safe and go back now! They thought I was a good guy to forego such activity by being prudent. I had no intention of being "entertained" by those ladies, but they did not know that. Incidentally, all of our combat wheeled vehicles had welded and braced channel iron on the front bumper designed to catch and break wire so that nobody would be decapitated.

And into Deutschland

My engineer battalion participated in the rapid crossing of France. We were attached to the 5th Armored "Victory" Division as engineer support. On the 11th of September 1944 we entered Germany at the little village of Wallendorf on the Our River. We were one of the initial U.S. combat units to enter Germany. We reinforced the existing Our River Bridge to accommodate the weight of heavy armored units. The German Siegfried Fortified Zone began on the other side of that river and contained many interconnecting underground tunnels that ran across our front. The Siegfried fortified zone's total length was some 400 miles, with pill boxes, tank obstacles, and dragon's teeth. All obstacles made of reinforced concrete located at considerable depth.

After making the initial Siegfried Line penetration, the tanks were ordered back out for a higher priority mission, leaving our battalion on September 19th/20th to defend and protect the bridge. High hills overlooked the bridge and we used that elevation to advantage in delivering devastating punishing firepower. The enemy combat engineer forces counterattacked and attempted to demolish the Our River Bridge, however, we successfully out-gunned them. The U.S. 5th Corps Commander, Lt. General Leonard Gerow, (3 stars) ordered us to reorganize as infantry and defend and hold that bridge at all costs. The enemy certainly tried to take it back, but thank God we prevailed!

In addition to our rifle fire, we used all of our 30- and 50-caliber machine guns to protect OUR Wallendorf Bridge. Every fourth or fifth cartridge of continuous belted ammunition contained a white hot tracer bullet; this was true for both German and U.S. machine gun ammunition. This insured that the shooter was concentrating his fire on the appropriate target. At times, German infantry and their combat engineers would destroy buildings or bridges by burning to preclude our offensive advance. It was impossible to determine which force or if both German and American weapons firing the tracers caused the Wallendorf village fires.

During this intense machine gun and rifle firefight by both sides, I noticed a very young child screaming, crying and running near the location of a former house. All that remained was the outline of the structure that was identified only by the red embers of what had been the walls of a farm structure.

I saw him stumble and fall into some of the burning embers as we were forcing the German forces from the little hamlet. We quickly got to the child and I noticed that some of his flesh hung down like thick molasses. Our medics gave him first aid and immediately evacuated him to a rear area field hospital. I often wondered if he survived those burns, and, if so, how he could function. This is but one example of the horrors of war. Not only do soldiers suffer but many thousands of innocent civilians as well. We did continue to hold this critical bridge until relieved by other U.S. combat forces.

In this type of combat our soldiers and officers all carried ammunition, water, rations, and heavy weapons up and down those hills. That's how the infantry coined the word "grunts" since they typically carry their weapons and all their other equipment into battle. In this operation we suffered three killed and eleven wounded.

Jack Davis RIP

In a later operation I lost my good friend Lt. Jack Davis, who sadly earned his second Purple Heart. Jack was hit with a Schmeisser 9mm. rapid fire machine pistol. He had 8 or 9 holes in his chest and stomach areas. When our medics, who wore large red cross markings on all four sides of their helmets, tried to treat and evacuate Jack, the German soldiers began firing on our medics as well. I commandeered a Sherman tank and used it to straddle Jack and pull him inside through the floor man-hole cover. The driver backed the tank out of that "killing zone" and we quickly got him to the battalion medical aid station. They immediately began giving him plasma and morphine. I held his head in my lap. He said to me that he was dying. I told him that he would be back in a field hospital soon and that the doctors and nurses would take good care of him. The ambulance departed and I was later told that he died en route to the field hospital. Jack was mortally wounded in Hitler's Siegfried line near Schmidt, Germany in March 1945. Helicopters had not been developed in time for use in WWII. I doubt that they could have saved Jack's life even if they had been available.

Jack and I had both been transferred to Company "A" commanded by Capt. Ware. I was assigned as the executive officer. That same day my company commander Captain Allison B. Ware received grievous leg wounds. One of his legs had to be amputated, which resulted in his retirement. I remember Jack Davis, Norman Watkins, Allison Ware, and Mike Cosella – all Purple Heart recipients – and others who gave so much of themselves in the defense of our country. Dear God, have mercy on their souls. Amen.

Lt. Frances Slanger

Some time in early October 1944 after our initial penetration into Germany's "Festung Europa," we were withdrawn and sent to Belgium to participate in a "Big Push," whatever that meant. While walking along a path to our bivouac area, a location close to the front line, some quartermaster soldiers were preparing to evacuate a number of dead U.S. soldiers' remains to a rear area temporary cemetery. All the dead looked the same. In need of a shave, dirty hands with weeks of dirt under the fingernails, filthy worn uniforms and the like. All looked the same except that one person was clean and soft of face, small delicate hands and in a clean uniform. On the right collar was a lieutenant's bar and on the other side was the medical caduceus with the letter "N" superimposed thereon. Then I saw her name. It was Lt. Frances Slanger.

During the Normandy campaign she had written an open letter to the widely distributed soldiers' newspaper, "Star and Stripes." The newspaper was the combat soldiers' only way of knowing what was going on in the world. One segment was called "The Barracks Bag." A soldier could write and address his ideas/complaints to the editor. The comments with most merit were published.

Months before, from her field hospital bunk in Normandy, Lt. Slanger wrote an open letter something like this dedicated primarily to combat soldiers. She wrote that every day in her field hospital, a tent with a big red cross painted on the canvas top, there was a steady stream of incoming wounded soldiers. She wanted the troops to know that every soldier that she saw and treated received the same tender care and love as if every patient was her biological brother. Her brother was in fact an infantry soldier. It was a very emotional and heartfelt letter. She also said that all of the nurses, doctors, and related staff felt the same. She was the same Army nurse who was bathing Lt. Jack Davis when I visited him in a hospital tent in Normandy. That's when Davis told her that he was not completely bathed.

In his book, *Citizen Soldiers*, renowned historian Stephen Ambrose wrote, "Lt. Frances Slanger of the 45th Field Hospital expressed her feelings in an October letter addressed to *Stars and Stripes* but written to the troops: "You G.I.'s say we nurses rough it. We wade ankle deep in mud. You have to lie in it. We have a stove and coal....In comparison to the way you men are taking it, we can't complain, nor do we feel that bouquets are due us....It is to you we doff our helmets.

"We have learned about our American soldier and the stuff he is made of. The wounded don't cry. Their buddies come first. The patience and determination they show, the courage and fortitude they have is sometimes awesome to behold. It is a privilege to receive you and a great distinction to see you open your eyes and with that swell American grin, say, 'Hi-ya, babe.'"

Slanger was killed the following day by an artillery shell. She was one of seventeen Army nurses killed in combat.

Nurse Slanger had given her life when the hospital received German army shelling. I'd like to think it was by accident. Many years later the military named in her honor a hospital ship, the U.S. Army Hospital Ship Frances Y. Slanger. It was later retired, and the task today of transporting military wounded is performed by helicopters and then air transport to the U.S.

V-1 Flying Bombs

On 29 November 1944, at about dusk, our battalion was operating out of a thick forested area. Company officers routinely inspected the combat outposts, especially at night. These outposts were always manned with at least two soldiers. This night I was checking the various company outposts to insure that:

- Adequate ammunition was on site

- At least one soldier was awake and alert

- The sound power alert telephone and radios were operational to company headquarters

- Machine gun muzzles were channeled between two guide stakes for night firing

- Any suspicious enemy activity to be promptly reported via phone or radio

- Adequate rations and water were on hand

- As best I could, evaluate their emotional and physical condition

As I was carefully approaching one of the other outposts, I head the distinct sound of a German V-1 "Vengeance" unmanned, thousand-pound flying bomb. As long as the pulse jet engine continued to function, you knew that it was likely programmed for London or the Port of Antwerp, Belgium. However, if damaged by ground fire, it could fall and explode anywhere. In the past few months, a number of those V-1's had passed over us flying at between 500 and 1,000 feet.

Antwerp was the logistics key required to support the continued forward advance operations of all allied forces. Otherwise ammunition, rations, medical supplies, troop replacements, and fuel would have to travel all the way from the Normandy beaches through France and Belgium to support us.

General Eisenhower's logistical forces had begun receiving some initial supplies through the large Antwerp port. At the same time his major subordinate field commanders were focusing their interests on the Rhine river, the last major natural obstacle, objective, and prize on the way to Berlin. The port's operations had been hindered by Hitler's V-1 flying bombs. The Supreme Commander wanted combat troops to fire on the V-1s to preclude their detonation in London and Antwerp.

Some other combat unit must have damaged this particular V-1 since I heard the engine sputtering, and then no more sound for a few seconds. Then there was a tremendous explosion. The concussion propelled me some 20-30 feet into a large tree. My knees were bleeding and I had a lot of pain in my back. The official battalion history reported that our medical personnel treated 65 men seriously wounded that night. People like myself who could still function were not included in that number, nor did we seek medical attention since the medics were overwhelmed with head wounds, fractured limbs, and the like.

Only the most seriously wounded were treated and then evacuated to a field hospital. The following morning we were able to fully determine the extent of damage. The blast pressure destroyed or severely damaged trucks, Jeeps, generators, tents, and some field cooking equipment. Again, I was very lucky. I did not officially report my injuries or seek the Purple Heart, due to the recent injuries and/or deaths of Mike Cosella, Allison Ware, Norman Watkins, Jack Davis, Arlan Bond, and other brother officers who all joined the battalion at the same time.

Hitler's V-2 Rocket

This weapon was designed to destroy the civilian population's will to resist in England, and in the major civilian centers on the European continent. The German V-2 rocket flew beyond the earth's atmosphere and could not be attacked by aircraft. Once fired, they were unstoppable. The only counter measure was to destroy the missiles before they were launched. To destroy them while they were still in (secret) production, in storage, or on their mobile launch pads. Or if fortunate, we could destroy their secret fixed launch sites.

Combat troops could see in the distance their telltale vapor rocket trails and used a triangulation technique to locate and bring field artillery fire on the launch sites, from azimuth readings. This information was transmitted by field telephone or radio to our artillery firing locations. Aircraft pilots also reported similar intelligence information. German troops were able to quickly set up, fire, and immediately disperse to alternate firing positions. We never knew if our provided data resulted in any launch facility destructions or not.

In November 1944, the Army organized combined task elements of armor motorized infantry, 50-caliber anti-aircraft, and engineer demolition platoons to punch through enemy civilian villages and small towns before the Germans could organize them into defensive strong point fighting positions. We would approach a German village, and if we were not fired upon, we would demand to see the mayor (burgomaster). He would be given an ultimatum to have all of the obstacles (fallen trees, mines, booby traps, trucks, busses, cars, wagons, and debris) removed from the roadway within a specified time. All able-bodied civilians and horses were to be used to meet the deadline. Failure would result in shelling and automatic firing on the town. Meanwhile, we would continue our advance to the next hamlet with the same demands.

When German army resistance was encountered or civilians fired at us, the lead tank would take one side of the street under fire, while the following tank would begin firing on the opposite side. At the same time the antiaircraft guns would employ the same technique. They would begin firing at street level from the town entrance and continue to the far end. Then elevate the firing at upper levels. The devastation was overwhelming.

Very soon white flags would appear. Prisoners were taken, the burgomaster gave into our demands and conditions, and on we would go. Our engineers were used to fill deep road craters with our bulldozers and road graders. When road defiles were encountered, our heavy engineer equipment performed a vital role in overcoming such obstacles promptly by bridging them and permitting the advance to continue.

The Battle of the Bulge

The overall war advanced so quickly that we began to run out of fuel, rations, and essential logistical supplies. We then had to halt and await for supplies to catch up with us. Then came the terrible cold weather with snow and freezing conditions. No overcoats or galoshes were available for some combat units. Intelligence estimates advised that under strength enemy forces were incapable of major offensive operations. New inexperienced divisions arrived from America. All seemed relatively secure.

On December 17th, the 254th Engineer Combat Battalion was supporting the 99th Infantry Division, newly arrived from the U.S. This was their first time in the line. It was believed that they were in a relatively quiet sector. Army intelligence assumed that, due to snow and ice, the German Army was in a holding position. They would likely be receiving replacements and equipment in preparation for the expected allied offensive operations in the following spring.

Allied intelligence and operational headquarters staffs thought it was safe to thin the troops on line and resort to reconnaissance and patrol activity to keep the enemy off balance.

My battalion had been assigned the typical winter tasks of improving and maintaining roads, bridges, conducting engineer reconnaissance, mine/demolition removal, sanding slick and ice-frozen roads, and potable water supply to all organizations in our area.

The battalion operated in a wooded area southeast of Bullingen, Belgium. On December 16th, Hitler unleashed some 300,000 mobile German troops against thin Allied opposition including some inexperienced U.S. infantry units. This was the onset of what became known as the Battle of the Bulge. For this operation Hitler had pulled some crack units from the Russian front to further insure his objective of splitting the Allied lines and capturing the critical Allied logistical port of Antwerp. He also employed a number of the newly-developed Tiger Royal tanks armed with the high velocity 90mm antitank gun.

Our smaller American M-4 Sherman tanks with their 75mm main guns were no match for the more powerful enemy weapons. Unexpectedly our infantry was also facing some of the best SS Stormtroopers, German airborne, and other special units. A number of experienced U.S. divisions were also badly under strength.

About midnight on the 16th our battalion was alerted to reorganize for an infantry mission in the Bullingen area of Belgium.

When attacked by stronger enemy tank infantry units, their tanks penetrated our lines. However, we stopped their infantry. But on the third attack, they overran us.

The battalion fought with courage, distinction, and determination even though outgunned and outnumbered. I was again very lucky.

It was little known at the time that the Germans even employed English-speaking German soldiers dressed in U.S. uniforms to get behind our lines.

The enemy would not have turned the course of the war, but they could have prolonged it and caused tragic losses. They had counted on bad weather to keep Allied air power from joining the battle. When the weather broke and the bombers and fighters were able to attack, the German assault was turned back, and at immense costs, especially to the enemy.

Once the Battle of the Bulge was contained, all combat troops were extremely security conscious. Since German soldiers had been wearing our uniforms, we would not accept or trust any group of guys just because they were in our uniforms without first verifying specifically who they were.

As an example. On roads or trails leading into our area, we dug 30- and 50-caliber machine guns into the bottom of roadside ditches along the entry road/trail. The muzzle would be about 6" above the road surface. Several hundred feet ahead of the machine gun; on the opposite site of the road we would have a soldier dug deep into the ditch. Should foot troops or a convoy approach, that outpost guard (opposite side from the guns) would command the approaching troops to halt. And they had better stop or the machine guns would begin firing. Once stopped, the outpost soldier would ask a single approaching soldier where he was from in the U.S. Then, for ex- ample, if that person said he was from New York, our soldier might ask, "Who is Joe DiMaggio?" He had better know that Jolting Joe was a baseball player from New York.

We did this type of questioning because the Germans had obtained the various passwords and countersigns. If you said California, you could be asked to name the location of the state capital, the governor's name, or something similar.

Foot Protection

During this time we lost some officers and soldiers to trench foot. This is a condition where wet feet freeze with loss of blood circu- lation, causing the toes or foot to turn black, sometimes resulting in amputation. When the feet are soaked for days in ice and snow, one can quickly become a victim of trench foot. A treatment was devised that helped. It was to require soldiers to remove their boots and rub their feet. Each person had to have a pair of dry socks. Then the wet socks would be "wrung out" and placed inside the uniform around the body to dry out (for the next sock exchange). This was very serious business. In all fairness, some personnel on a gun, an outpost, or working on a critical bridge repair, could not remove or change socks. The removal of boots for foot massage, change of socks with bare feet, and the potential for enemy unexpected intervention at any time for some people, made this an option that couldn't work for everyone.

During the Battle of the Bulge, the Army lost so many infantry soldiers – dead, wounded and captured – that General Eisenhower ordered that any rear area soldiers, including soldiers who volunteered for infantry combat duty, could not be denied that service, even if declared "essential" by any commanding officer. These soldiers, of all races, who had been working as clerks and logistics aides, were given a few weeks special infantry training and then assigned to combat infantry units. We received some very dedicated soldiers under the provisions of General Eisenhower's order.

As the Battle of the Bulge was drawing to a successful U.S. conclusion, our Engineer Group chaplain was able to come to our battalion to celebrate Mass. It was still freezing and deep snow everywhere. The word was out that the priest would be saying Mass, and the guys were assembling in a wooden area. The Jeep hood served as an altar. There was a large attendance, and I suspect that almost all Catholic soldiers in the battalion were present.

The father announced that there would not be sufficient time for him to hear confessions since he also had to travel to other battalions. He said that in very unusual circumstances that now existed, we could be granted conditional absolution with the full intention of going to Confession at the first opportunity. Mass was then celebrated, and we all received the Holy Eucharist.

A month or so later, when the war was much more in our favor, the chaplain was able to return for Mass. Human nature being what it is, I noticed that there was a somewhat smaller number of men attending this time. When the risk of life and limb is highest and the Sacraments are available, Mass attendance is high. When the danger has passed, and all things righted by some people, unfortunately, God is forgotten.

Recognition

One of the most significant events for me was the recognition by the War Department of what our battalion did at the Battle of the Bulge. This is it:

From War Department General Order
No.32 Washington, D.C. 23 April 1945

The 254ᵗʰ Engineer Combat Battalion is cited for extraordinary heroism in action against an armed enemy on 17 December 1944 in Belgium. Early in the morning of 17 December 1944, the battalion was ordered to take up a defensive position on the corps' right flank. Although armed only with small arms, machine guns, and rocket launchers, and completely unsupported, the battalion successfully resisted several vicious attacks by armored infantry and tanks. When finally overrun physically by enemy tanks, the battalion continued its determined and heroic resistance from successive positions for a period of nine hours before relief finally arrived. This gallant and courageous action enabled successful measures to be taken to secure the safety of the corps' right flank, permitted the evacuation of large stores of gasoline and rations sorely needed by the enemy, and denied him the use of three vital routes of approach. The determination, heroism, and esprit de corps displayed by the individual officers and men of the battalion in this successful action against a powerful enemy armored force, despite severe losses, prevented the enemy from penetrating the corps' rear areas and contributed materially to the ultimate failure of his counterattack. It reflects great credit on the 254ᵗʰ Engineer Combat Battalion and is in keeping with the finest tradition of the military service.

Tuskegee Pilots

During the same period, the Tuskegee Institute, a black college in Alabama had previously trained fighter P-51 pilots who were deployed to Europe. They provided escort for B-17 Flying Fortress raids on Germany. When performing that duty, it was said that they never lost a single B17 Bomber to enemy fighter aircraft. The Germans initially remarked that black pilots would not fight. So those P-51 pilots, I was told, painted the nose and tail yellow so that they could be easily identified. They were so good that later the bomber crews specifically requested them as their escorts. Today's military establishment has a significant number of black general officers. They are living examples of the tremendous equalizations evolution taking place in our pluralist society, being led by the Army.

At Last - a Diet Change

We had not had any real hot food with meat for a while; just cold army rations in little tuna fish-like tin cans. One day a soldier spied a live cow. He hung a hand grenade on one of the cow's horns and pulled the pin. After the explosion, the mess sergeant took charge and soon we all had fresh meat. The spoils of war. Now before getting upset over this, thousands of horses, cows, hens, and other farm animals were killed by aerial bombing, artillery shelling, mines and the like. Many animals suffered slow, brutal deaths due to combat, and virtually all of that meat rotted where the animals perished.

Re-Establishing Destroyed Roads

During late December 1944, the freezing weather began to thaw, the vintage little local asphalt trails and roads which were designed for bicycles, horse-drawn wagons, and light passenger autos quickly began to fail under the tremendous weight of tanks, tank destroyers, tracked artillery, and other heavy vehicles. In short order, the former roads were just miles of deep mud.

In order to solve that critical problem, we began building corduroy roads. An old, expedient technique was utilized. We cut down trees, cut the trees into logs, and then wired them together. Then rock and combat rubble were deposited on top of the logs to form a stable foundation. Many, many miles of corduroy roads were built by a number of engineer battalions, not only our unit. Without those pioneer roads, the Army would have been hopelessly bogged down and unable to continue the fight.

One evening at about dusk my company occupied a number of vacant German homes. The weather was quite cold and everyone was pleased that we would not be sleeping another night out in the open. By the time that we fueled our vehicles for the next day, posted security, and fed the troops, it was dark. I had now been transferred back to my original company, which was short of officers. The company commander, Captain Minor, First Sergeant Kovashich, and I finally got to spread out our sleeping bags for a well-deserved night's sleep. I was worn out from the stress of all the day's operations, the checking and coordination required in preparation for the next morning's early scheduled departure, and new operational requirements. It did not take long for me to fall into a deep sleep.

Hours later, for some unknown reason I awoke suddenly in complete darkness and fully alert. Don't know why but I quickly thrust both hands up, and discovered that I was grasping a wrist and hand. There was a scuffle and I called out "What's going on here?" The captain and the sergeant immediately awoke, and Sergeant Kovashich quickly grabbed a flashlight next to his bed roll and turned it on me. There was a young German woman who had been standing over me, pointing a Walther P-38 German Army pistol at my head a moment earlier. The darn thing was loaded. However, I did not know that when I grabbed that hand in the dark. What luck that it did not fire during the scuffle. That was more than "good luck" - more like a miracle!

I called the guard, took the pistol, and she was taken away. I don't know how she got into the house – maybe she was hiding in it when we occupied it – and why was she at my sleeping bag. Nor do I know what ever happened to her. Anyway, I knew that luck was still with me.

Near the end of the war, I was able to see Pete (my sister's fiancé) and I gave the P-38 pistol to him since I already had "liberated" a German Lugar pistol (serial number 7813). On Pete's troops ship returning from the war, he showed the pistol to some soldiers. Later while he was in the "chow line" someone got into Pete's barracks bag and stole that pistol. Possibly God intervened since that pistol could have caused a tragic event if not securely stored under lock and key.

Being Strafed

At the conclusion of the Battle of the Bulge, the Army was again on the attack into Germany. The battalion had been moving in the general direction of the Rhine River. It was early afternoon on the first day of 1945 and we had located a large area adequate to accommodate our men and their heavy equipment. We were deployed in a large circle on the periphery of a huge hill mass.

Soldiers were camouflaging our equipment when all of a sudden, a German Luftwaffe (Air Force) Messerschmitt ME 109 fighter aircraft began strafing our positions. There were U.S. anti-aircraft units in the vicinity positioned on the highest hilltops, armed with Quad 50-caliber machine guns (a gun mount with the four 50-caliber barrels in a cluster). When the strafing began, the pilot was flying at about 200 to 300 feet above the ground. We all began firing at the ME-109 with pistols, carbines, rifles, and our 30-caliber machine guns.

The pilot pulled up, banked into a turn around and came back strafing us again, into a hail of return ground firing. At the conclusion of the second pass, I noticed smoke coming from his cockpit. He was then attempting to gain altitude when I saw him open the canopy, roll out, and promptly activate his parachute. The flame from his aircraft immediately ignited the parachute and it completely burned in a flash. The aircraft crashed and exploded about a thousand feet from us. The pilot's body hit the ground on the side of a hill and tumbled down a slope near me.

A soldier closer than I got to the body first and quickly liberated his Mauser pistol. I was, however, able to get his flying jacket (too big for me) which I brought home from the war. In 1980 I gave the jacket to Owen Flannery, a young man who worked for me years later in San Francisco. Another soldier got the flight pants. By the way, none of our guys was hurt by the strafing.

As I reminisce about that day, I remember that the pilot was clean shaven. His fingernails were groomed, and he likely had slept in a warm, clean bed with sheets the previous night. Most likely he had enjoyed a well-prepared breakfast that morning. In contrast, infantry troops always needed a bath and longed for the warmth and better dining; certainly not possible for any combat troops.

Transporting Prisoners

One day I was leading a six-truck convoy loaded with prisoners.

Hundreds of male and maybe 20 female German Army prisoners. While riding they were all standing in the truck beds with 35 to 40 prisoners per trucks with straps around the outer periphery for their safety and to preclude escape. It took several hours to go to the rear, where a recently-constituted Belgium army unit operated a prisoner of war (PW) compound. It may have been comprised of the remnants of a former defeated Belgium Army unit. With a little training, they were running the camp, thereby releasing other Allied troops for combat duty.

After several hours on the road, the uniformed female prisoners who were likely medical and administrative personnel began to yell that they had to relieve themselves.

Since we had to take on a load of fuel in five gallon cans, ammo, rations, and other items on the return trip, I did not want to stop. Also, I had far too many prisoners to control if they all were let off the trucks. Then there were armed bands of German troops operating at night behind our lines, waiting to ambush convoys. I did, however, permit the women to dismount and take care of their needs. The men just had to hold it, or wet their pants. I was not going to risk my drivers, equipment, and supplies on our return to the battalion with the unnecessary dangers of a night enemy ambush.

After reloading the women, a few miles further along I was scanning the hills and I thought I saw some German soldiers with rifles under camouflage ponchos observing our convoy. I asked my drive if he had seen them. He said, "Lieutenant, you are so conscious of the enemy that you are seeing things." I stopped the convoy and asked every driver and guard the same question; all answered in the negative. I then became more sure! I always carried my M-1 Garand rifle, however, in my haste to question the other personnel, I only had my captured German Lugar pistol on my belt.

In a hurry I began going alone up the hill wondering if I was imagining things. When I got about one third of the way up the slope, I saw the first German soldier. From the prone position, he had his rifle pointed at me. My first reaction was to shoot first and then drop to the ground. At the same instant I saw another enemy soldier some 30 feet above the first soldier with his rifle trained on me. Then a third. I quickly realized that I was not going to out gun them alone with only a pistol.

I then shouted at the top of my voice "Krieg es fertig nix mit giwehr," which (in my German) meant "The war is finished. Don't use your rifles." It was not true, of course, but since they saw so many prisoners, they were not sure. I yelled it again and then one soldier stood up and tossed his rifle aside. A few moments later the second soldier followed suit, and finally the third.

Then I marched all three of them to my convoy, making sure that all of my guys saw that their lieutenant was on the ball, and that they had better be more alert in the future. Luck was still with me.

When we arrived at the PW camp to unload the prisoners, the Belgium guards began using the metal buckle ends of their belts to whip the prisoners as they entered the camp. As soon as I saw what was happening, I stopped that behavior immediately. I said, "You people did not capture them; how come you are so brave with unarmed prisoners?" I realized that German soldiers had brutalized Belgium soldiers and civilians when they first invaded their country but that was four years earlier and those particular German soldiers were likely already dead. We captured these former enemy person-nel – not those guards – and I was not going to permit them to be abused.

Now my mission was to insure that our trucks were reloaded for the return trip to the front as soon as possible. The U.S. supply segment of this facility was a member of a black quartermaster unit. They were located in a relatively safe rear area. Admittedly, all day long they were doing stevedore type work loading combat trucks that transported war supplies to the combat areas.

It seemed to me that they were taking their time in the loading process. All the while I was looking at my watch, realizing that if they didn't get us loaded quickly we would surely be driving back to the front in total darkness.

With the likelihood of German soldiers lying in wait for convoys, I finally called the person in charge and advised him to have his men speed up our loading. He said, "Lieutenant, if my men aren't loading your trucks fast enough, you and your men can load them trucks yo-self." I was furious but in that situation I agreed to have my men work with them to reduce the loading time. Fortunately, we returned to the battalion area without incident, just as it was getting dark.

Crossing the Rhine

The dramatic events on the Rhine River at the Luendorf Railroad Bridge at the town of Remagen has been well documented by WWII historians and an action-packed film. U.S. Brigadier General William Hogue (Basic Branch Corps of Engineers) was the commanding general of an armored combat command. The Rhine River is the widest, swiftest and deepest river in Germany and was the last major natural defensive barrier for Germany.

One of General Hogue's forward combat platoons approached the Rhine River in a patrol formation at Remagen, and discovered that the 1,400 foot railroad bridge spanning the Rhine was still intact. The lieutenant radioed that critical information to the rear where it promptly reached General Hogue.

German army combat engineers had previously installed adequate demolition charges to completely destroy the bridge. However, though neither side knew it, U.S. artillery shellfire fragments had severed certain major electrical demolition circuits. When the enemy observed American troops approaching, they detonated all circuits. Some charges exploded, other did not.

When General Hogue received the bridge status information he immediately ordered his combat platoon troops to cross the bridge and secure the far side. At the same time he ordered his armored units to quickly proceed to the bridge and expand the far shore bridgehead. Many vital structural components had been seriously damaged or destroyed and the bridge was extremely unstable. Concurrently, other U.S. combat engineers welders were trying to weld additional steel supportive components to the mortally damaged span.

Immediately the 5th Corps commanding general, Lt. Gen. Gerow, ordered our engineer battalion to construct a floating backup bridge. Since it was doubtful that the railroad bridge could be saved, our construction began around the clock on the 21st of March 1945and we completed the operation on the 22nd. It took the expenditure of 45,000 man-hours, establishing a record of 1328 feet of floating treadway bridge. This historic achievement made it the longest tactical bridge ever constructed under fire.

The 254th Engineer Combat Battalion selected a near shore site at

Niederbreisig to handle the far shore of our floating treadway bridge where the traffic would exit at the village of Honnigen on the far shore.

At this time the German air force had developed the first combat jet fighter aircraft. It was a twin-engine plane identified as the ME-262. It was rushed into production, and, fortunately for us, their pilots had little training with their bombing-strafing armaments. They came close but never hit our bridge. Also, we had our guys in small boats throwing TNT and hand grenades in the water on both sides of our bridge to insure that enemy underwater demolition men could not destroy our bridge. No sooner was our bridge completed when the Remagen Railroad Bridge collapsed and fell into the Rhine, injuring and killing a number of soldiers from another U.S. engineer battalion. An official army photo of our bridge depicts the length and importance of this span. We were handling all types of tanks, artillery, half tracks, antiaircraft guns, and tank destroyer units.

During this construction, our battalion headquarters was located in the large Rhineland Hotel only a few hundred feet from the bridge construction site. The hotel covered all four sides of a complete city block. Its basement however was extremely small in relationship to the scale of the hotel. Some of our soldiers had gifted noses. They could detect alcohol much like a mine detector can pinpoint an explosive device.

Our soldiers discovered that the true basement's footprint was the same size as the hotel. They made the discovery when they took it upon themselves to knock down one of the basement walls. There they uncovered a huge treasure trove of thousands of cases of expensive Rhine wine. The German government wanted it saved for celebration purposes at their winning of the war.

With this discovery, we stacked hundred of cases at the bridge site. Every tank, artillery gun crew, half track, tank destroyer, every truckload of infantry soldiers - everybody was given a case of Rhine wine. Thank goodness the wine was not discovered until after our bridge was completed!

At this location, the Rhine River had a number of boats, barges, and other water craft moored at the near shore. Just as our bridge construction was completed and our tanks began crossing our span, I climbed down the riverbank and entered one of the vessels. There I discovered a large Nazi flag. I quickly took possession of that war souvenir and brought it back home at war's end to be added to my other war mementos. In 2007, I presented that flag to Jesse Chudnofsky, whose family had lost many members in the Holocaust. His parents have been very special family friends of ours for more than twenty years.

What a Surprise

After crossing the Rhine River, we were transferred (on paper) from the U.S. First Army to General Patton's Third Army as of 6 May 1945. Gen. Patton wanted to continue his attack to capture Berlin. This would have surely resulted in a high cost of U.S. lives and equipment. However, the Big Three leaders – Churchill, Stalin, and Truman – agreed to let Russia have the German capital. Accordingly, General Eisenhower ordered General Patton to proceed to Pilsen, Czechoslovakia. It was reported that some elements of the German army had possibly begun to desert since the Russians were less than one hundred miles from Berlin.

While en route to Pilsen, now a city in the Czech Republic, the U.S. Army encountered very stiff resistance at certain objectives. Other operations met uncoordinated resistance. Understandably German soldiers did not want to be captured or taken prisoner by the Soviet army. They well understood that the Russians would be very severe in the treatment of their enemy.

This took place on or about May 5th 1945, only three days before the formal end of the war in Europe on May 8th, when we were only 25 miles from Pilsen. I was leading the battalion convoy when I noticed a blind curve ahead. As I entered that curve, coming towards me was a long column of some 20 German tanks! What a shock to be killed or taken prisoner during the last few days of the war.

Just as I and my Jeep driver "Rebel" were about to bail out of the Jeep, I realized that all of the German tank commanders were fully exposed, riding high in the turrets. Plus, each tank displayed a white flag with their road lights on in the daytime."Rebel" I said, "they are surrendering!"

The first tank approached my stopped Jeep. The commander saluted me and said in English that they wanted to surrender. I told him to continue driving in the direction they were headed, and that further on some other U.S. Army organization would take charge of his men and their equipment. We saluted each other and we proceeded on the Pilsen without further incident.

Later I discovered that my experience was not that unique. Similar actions had occurred to some other units.

On our arrival in Pilsen, we were greeted as liberators amidst music, dancing and Pilsen beer. We met the Russian troops there with much handshaking, hugs, backslapping, and good cheer. The Russian troops I saw were all Mongolians (Asian in facial appearance). The Russian soldiers were mystified when watching our soldiers brush their teeth. They had no knowledge of toothpaste or toothbrushes. Also, wristwatches were only for senior leaders. For socks they tore up bed sheets into long strips and wrapped them around the foot and ankle before placing the foot in the boot.

They had been issued U.S. invasion currency and quickly purchased used or new tooth brushes and tooth paste from our guys. These health items were included in our regular food ration, and were of course not for sale! Wristwatches also became a very pricey item. They could not understand how the ordinary American basic soldier could have a wristwatch. It did not take long for some of our soldiers I'm sure to become "unofficial businessmen." Unknown to us, the Russians printed bogus U.S. currency in denominations that our government had never printed.

Short-lived Occupation Duty

My battalion participated in the joint U.S.-Soviet occupation of Pilsen during the period of May 11th to the 22nd. We supervised some 3,000 former elite German SS Storm Troop prisoners in their repair and rehabilitation of utilities that they had destroyed prior to our arrival.

Centuries ago, the King of Bohemia ordered that certain designated cities would produce specified goods/services for the kingdom. Pilsen is a beautiful old world city that was tasked to provide beer for the kingdom. For refrigeration they dug into a nearby mountain and by so doing obtained a constant cold temperature. Their beer quickly became word famous. Today the word "Pilsen Type Beer" is used in some advertising. In WWII our battalion requisitioned that beer to supplement the meal ration.

On May 22nd, the battalion was ordered to leave Pilsen and return to France to construct redeployment tent camps to send recently arrived troops that had little or no combat time for participation in the Pacific War.

A day before I had been introduced to a local medical doctor. This day she asked me to hide her in my covered Jeep trailer and let her out anywhere in Germany, Belgium, or France. I told her that would be in violation of orders, and that I could not do that. Europe was already full of displaced nationals. I commented that she should be happy to be liberated and free. She said as soon as we departed, the Russians will stay and her country would be a part of the Soviet Union. Like most Americans, I thought that the Russians were our friends and allies. Little did our national leaders understand that the Cold War would soon be on us. That doctor was a very wise woman. I always wondered what happened to her.

Like most young single men in Europe during WWII, the troops met young ladies at the Red Cross canteens, at the United Service Organizations in England (USOs), and others across Europe. Some soldiers became pen pals with those ladies, and a large number of the women became war brides. I had a little address book of names and addresses of a few of those young ladies. However, I never wrote to any of them.

During our few operational days in Paris, I met an attractive young lady and my captain noticed me recording her long forgotten address. One day after the Battle of the Bulge, Captain Minor asked me if I had been in touch with the Parisian lady. If not, did I intend to contact her later? I told him that I had no such intentions, and that I had a lady friend in the U.S. Her name was Grace Hardy, and I called her "Toodie." While not engaged, we had a sort of understanding. At this point, he asked if I'd give him the French lady's name and address.

Captain Minor was likely in his early thirties. The lady was probably 20 years old. He wrote her many letters over the months. When we arrived Pilsen and the war ended, he told me that he had proposed marriage and that she had accepted. He asked me to be his best man. The wedding would take place in a Catholic church in Paris. He also invited Lt. Edwin Shafter to the wedding. The two of us were given a three-day pass and received permission to use a Jeep for the trip.

This was the first wedding that I had ever attended. We had only recently liberated Paris nine months previously and, as a result, Americans were still highly regarded. After the church ceremony, the bride's family had a wonderful reception and dinner for all. There was one goblet for white wine, another for red, one for champagne and one for liqueurs. And, of course, many different French food entrees! What an experience for a young man like me who came from a middle class working family. I had never experienced such elegant food and drink before. Nor have I since.

After the church wedding and during this celebration, Captain Minor participated in too many toasts. The French were much more accustomed to alcohol than we. At one point, Aimes was having difficulty, so Ed and I put him on top of a bed, removed his shoes while he slept, with his bride in tears next to the bed.

At the dinner I had been seated next to the bride's cousin. Another attractive young lady. I don't remember her name, either! We danced and had a very nice time. As Ed and I were leaving, I thanked her for her company and said that if she knew a nice restaurant I'd be pleased to take her to dinner before I returned to Pilsen.

She said that she would very much like that; however, she said that she was "very correct." I did not understand just what that meant. So I said. I also am very correct! She said no dinner date, but would I like a "rendezvous"? I had no idea what to expect. So I said okay. She replied that we should meet at the Metro station in front of the Opera Building at 5:30 the next afternoon.

I was there at 5:20 waiting. At 5:30 she exited the Metro. We shook hands, talked about the lovely wedding, the dancing, food, and that day's weather. Then about ten minutes later, she offered me her hand and said, "au revoir,"and walked away. That's the last I saw of her. A quick French lesson.

For the wedding Ed and I shared a Paris hotel room. We had been given written instructions how to get from our hotel to the church and the Metro transfer stations to and from the wedding. We were all pressed, dressed with our medals and all. At the dinner, due to our celebrating, we lost the metro instructions! Imagine the challenge now of returning to our hotel at two in the morning. Despite our poor use of French words, with the help of the locals and relying on gestures, we finally got ourselves back to the hotel.

About the year 2000, I heard that Captain Minor had been a construction contractor after leaving the Army in 1945, and that he had since passed away. His wife had become a registered nurse where they were living. If she is still alive, as of this writing, she must be in her late eighties.

Pacific Redeployment Camp Construction

A number of combat divisions, each having a strength of about 15,000 men, arrived in Europe during the latter part of the war against the Nazis, and they had little actual combat operational experience. Accordingly, most of those personnel had low service points when victory in Europe (VE Day) was declared on May 8th 1945. For that reason they were immediately scheduled for redeployment to the Pacific for participation in the expected final assault on Japan. They were to be sent home, given 30 days leave, and then redeployed to the Pacific Theater. Combat units like mine with high points were scheduled for occupation duty in Germany and Austria.

In preparation for their redeployment, our engineer battalion was ordered to promptly depart Pilsen and within three days return to France in the extensive "Oise" Champagne District. On arrival, we moved into a large uncultivated area. The mission, using German prisoners and our soldiers, was to construct a series of redeployment tent camps to accommodate that large troop redeployment. Those camps were given the names of popular cigarettes. The tent camp we constructed was identified as camp Lucky Strike. Others were called Pall Mall, Camels, and the like. Those camps were constructed by other engineer battalions.

The very high service point "old timers," WWII Reserve Officers, enlistees and draftees were promptly discharged and were in the United States when the atomic bombs ended the war in the Pacific. The same category of personnel in Europe were delayed in separation since their numbers far exceeded the capability of ocean transport. A point quota system was established for their eventful U.S. return.

Many of the Victory Parades were performed by "low services point" troops in the U.S. that were being assembled for the expected invasion of Japan. What good fortune for them. Then many of them were promptly discharged. The vast majority of combat high service point troops had experienced the horrors of war and wanted to return home promptly. They opted out of the parades and related celebrations.

With 88 combat points I could elect to remain for occupation duty, command a company or return to the U.S. I was assigned as the commanding officer of one of the company size units. The tent camps consisted of sleeping tents, mess tents, shower units, latrines, and large tents for orientation/administration/evening movies and medical support. Having served as a 1st lieutenant for a major part of the war, I was pleased to be in a captain's assignment again. I expected to be promoted to captain after a reasonable period of demonstrating my command ability. Then the war department ordered that no promotions were to be awarded since the size and composition of the post war army would be greatly reduced.

All of our original National Guard troops who had been ordered to duty in 1940 had very high point numbers; well over a hundred. They all elected to return home for discharge. People like myself had a lot of points but not quite enough to immediately go home, so soldiers in my category were retained in Europe to be part of the occupation army. With a few more points in due time, we also could return home for separation/discharge, or remain for occupation duty.

At the completion of the Lucky Strike redeployment camp, I elected not to participate in the occupation of Germany, but to return home. The purpose was to pursue my education and determine what else life held in store for me. Meanwhile, my brother Bub had already returned home from duty with the B-29 heavy bombers of the Army Air Corps on Guam, and was discharged. My buddy Pete, who was engaged to my sister Anne, had wired my parents requesting that they take her to the port of debarkation so that they could be married on his return. I had been assured that my engineer job in Washington was awaiting my return. In addition, I wondered what if anything would or could develop with my former lady friend I called "Grace." I therefore awaited my turn for a space on the next available troopship.

A Tragedy on the Voyage Home

My return transportation was provided aboard the U.S. Cody Victory Liberty ship in December 1945 with some 2,000 troops on-board. With terribly crowded conditions, with men seasick below decks, limited toilet facilities, and other problems, in my view she was severely overloaded.

Some two days short of our Hampton Roads, Virginia debarkation port with demobilization at Camp Patrick Henry, the ship stopped in mid-ocean calm waters. Everybody on board was yelling "Get this bucket on to Hampton Roads." After a while the ship's captain announced over the ship's public address system "Would a Catholic officer report to the bridge immediately?" So up to the bridge I went.

The captain promptly took me into a little operating room. He said that a young sergeant that I did not know was dying. He wanted me to say a mass for him. I would then have to write the condolence letter to his parents. I explained that only an ordained priest could celebrate a mass. However, I had some Catholic soldiers onboard that I knew. With them I would say the Rosary, the Act of Contrition, and other appropriate prayers in his behalf. The patient was on the operating table and I saw the incision. His fingernails were turning color; he was already dead.

The medical technician told me that he had a severe appendix attack, that they had packed him with ice in hopes of having his operation at the Hampton Roads military hospital. But things had gone very badly and they had to operate immediately while at sea. I asked to talk to the doctor who had performed the surgery. The technician stated that there was no doctor on board and that they had tried to save his life as best they could. The patient was young and very handsome.

With much thought, after our prayers I drafted a condolence letter to his parents. I still have a copy of that letter. I told them that I did not know their son since there were thousands of men aboard the Cody Victory Liberty Ship en route home. There was no purpose in telling them that there was no doctor onboard. It was enough to say that when their son became ill with a very serious appendicitis infection, that the ship's entire medical staff was immediately placed at his disposal. I also told them that the seas were calm and the ship's captain had stopped the vessel to eliminate or minimize any potential movement. I explained that I assembled a group of Catholic soldiers and that we said the act of contrition, the rosary and other prayers for the repose of his soul. They were given my name, address, and local telephone number should they want to contact me further. They never wrote or telephoned me to acknowledge my letter. I could only imagine their tremendous grief of losing their son on the way home after surviving the war!

Photographs

My father, age 60

My father's crucifix

My father's medical ID tag 1918

My maternal grandfather - Mr. Bruen

Me crowning grammar school May Queen

Country relatives; me in white sailor hat

Aunt Belle

Country house during Great Depression

My parents' retirement residence

Grace and me in early 1943

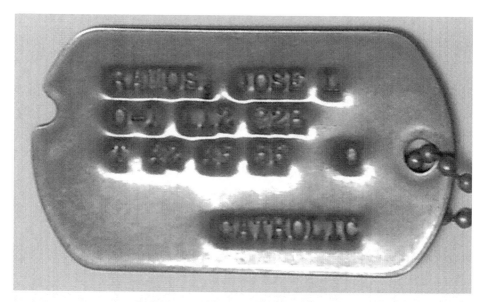

My enlisted ID tag

Ed Shaffer, Jack Davis and me in England

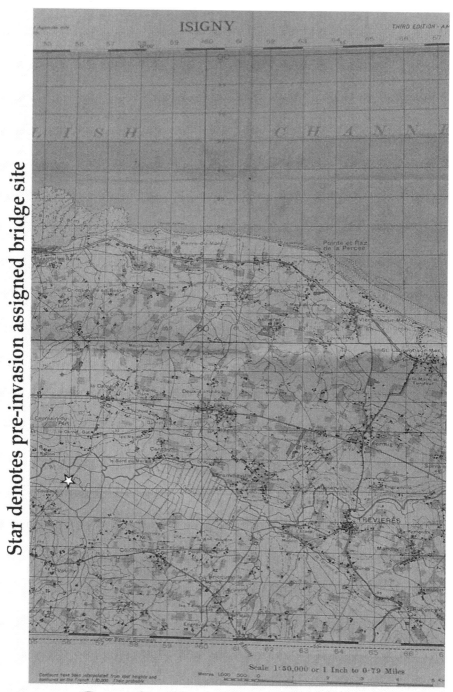

Star denotes pre-invasion assigned bridge site

Omaha Beach – 6 June 1944

Currency of D-Day invasion troops

1951 visit to Normandy Beach

1993 visit to Normandy Beach

Sanding a frozen road

Safe method of anti-tank mine removal

Our company after the Bulge
I'm fourth from left in second row

Pete and I somewhere in Belgium

The bridge over the Rhine
A proud engineering achievement

Near shore-Niederbreisig; far shore Honnigen

USS hospital ship Frances Y. Slanger
Named after a very dedicated nurse

The Normandy Cemetery - 1993
The grave of Lt. Norman Watkins

"Captain" Robert in his jeep

The children in their Davy Crockett outfits

Lt. Col. Clock and I inspecting the troops

Site of pre-loaded demolition trucks
(near Danube River)

Building the troops' confidence

Demolition confidence training

Night demolitions training

**Lt. Gen. George P. Hays and Grace
and me at my award ceremony**

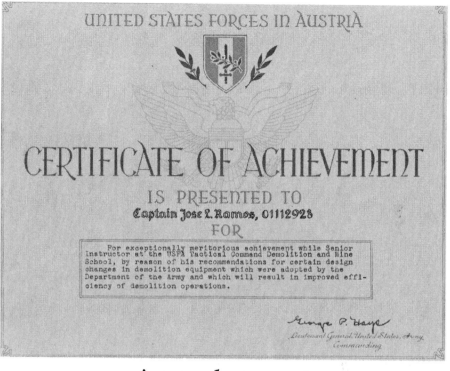

A proud moment

Debris in river bed needing to be cleared

Stroudsburg, Pa. bridge washed away

Typical Korean winter icicles

7th Division chapel ready for dedication

**Paraguayan soldiers working barefoot
on bridge component**

Helping priests build homes for the poor

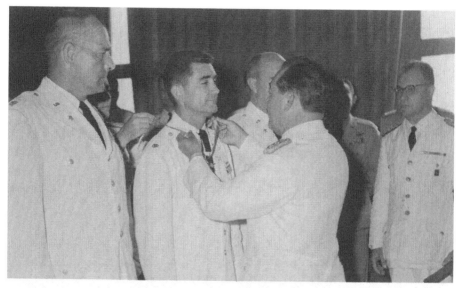

Receiving a decoration in Paraquay

**We replaced bridge destroyed by rebels
with a floating military span**

Ft. Benning bridge to parachute drop zone

Same bridge destroyed in making of "The Green Berets" movie

Farewell roast illustration of the assumption of my Civilian "Command"

French Army Cavalry Museum - 1993
Standing before German Tiger Royal tank the type used in the Battle of the Bulge

Home at Last

The ship arrived, and after deboarding we were all given a steak dinner at Camp Patrick Henry then our final leave payment, discharge papers, and a ticket for the train ride home.

When returning to the U.S. not a part of a major unit, such personnel were identified as casuals in transit. For us there were no flags, no parades, no speeches, only mustering out administrative procedures. Each soldier was given a little cloth patch that displayed an eagle indicating that the individual was en route home after discharge and was going back to civilian life. A little lapel eagle pin generally referred to as the "Ruptured Duck" was also issued for wear on the lapel of a business suit or jacket. And now a civilian once more.

However, the federal government required that certain officers were automatically assigned upon relief from active duty to reserve force units, with retention on those rolls until age 60/62 (unless medically unfit). At that time I did not give much thought to the reserve requirement.

Returning home and being with my parents, other family members, and friends was a true joy. There were lots of kisses from mom and dad with much backslapping from other family members and friends. Everyone was also anxious to see the German helmet, the Lugar pistol, German artillery binoculars, Nazi flag, and other liberated enemy memorabilia items that I had acquired.

It was customary during WWII for families that had sons serving in the defense of our country, to display an emblem type flag. For each family member serving there would be a single blue star on a white background with red border. Since both Bub and I were in the service, our parents displayed two blue stars on their flag. A gold star displayed on the flag signified the combat death of a family member while serving our country.

Now that I was the last son home, they removed that flag from the front window. A small flag can be seen in the window on the right side of my parents' entry door.

The 254th Engineer Combat Battalion on return to the US was inactivated as a federal force and rejoined the Michigan National Guard, It was later redesignated as the 107th Engineer Combat Battalion as a part of the Michigan governor's military National Guard force.

When I went off to war the Ramos family resided in a brick row house in Washington. During the war years, Mom and Dad sold that home and purchased a lovely separate residence on a beautiful lot in Silver Springs, Maryland on the outskirts of the District.

As mentioned earlier, my brother Bub had already been discharged from the U.S. Army Air Corps, and had returned home and was making plans to continue his college education at the University of Maryland. The campus was close and he could continue living at home to avoid the costs of living on campus.

My sister Anne and my now-brother-in-law, Pete, were already married, and temporarily stayed at our parents home while awaiting to occupy nearby veterans housing. The housing was modified converted former federal government military barracks that were reassembled in Sligo Creek Parkway. The parkway is a beautiful area, however, the young families that lived there called it "Splinter Village," because the housing was all former military frame barracks.

When Anne and Pete were married, I was still overseas and on my return they had moved to "Splinter Village." One day my mother told me that Anne became pregnant on her honeymoon. Anne took great pride in preparing Pete's breakfast before his morning departure for work as a plumber's apprentice. One morning while Anne was fixing Pete's breakfast she remarked to mom that the smell of bacon, eggs, and other breakfast items gave her a strange feeling in her stomach. In due time, one morning Pete called me, telling me that Anne was having severe labor pains and that en route to the hospital he would pick me up to accompany them posthaste. As I recall, Pete's car was a two-door Plymouth coup. The three of us occupied the bench seat and took off for the hospital, happy and excited. Pete drove, and when safe to do so, even through red lights since Anne said that the baby might be born on the way. Accordingly, I took off my white tee shirt and would wave it out the window to warn and signal other motorists of our priority. I'm sure Pete had the car headlights and horn in play. I don't remember that part except that at one intersection I lost the undershirt!

On arrival at the hospital, a nurse told Pete, "Relax, there is no hurry," that since it was Anne's first baby, the infant (today Michael Peter, in his late 60's) would not be born for sometime. She said for us to go to a local restaurant, have breakfast, buy a newspaper and then return to join other would-be fathers in the waiting room.

On our return from breakfast, the nurse told Pete, "Congratulations, Mr. Peter you are the father of a son. Little Michael Peter and Mrs. Peter are both fine." That was a very memorable event for me. I will never forget Michael's birth.

Career Decision

At this time I was 23 years old and living at home. I knew that my civilian job as a member of a field survey team with the District of Columbia Surveyors Office was waiting for me. They wanted my return and at the same time I planned to pursue my college engineering education. Some of the professional engineers suggested that I could do both as they had done. Work with them in my daytime civilian job and enroll in college courses at night. It would take longer to graduate, but I would be supporting myself. I thought that was an acceptable option so I returned to work and enrolled in night school in pursuit of my interrupted educational goal. During this time my plate was full with work and school and I had no social life at all.

One day, I decided to telephone Grace Hardy's parents home. Grace answered the phone and I asked her if she was still single, and if so, did she have a special boy friend. She said that there was no special boyfriend. I therefore invited her to accompany me to the movies. We enjoyed each other's company. Her parents, Mr. and Mrs. Hardy, had always been very nice to me and before the war, had invited me to Sunday dinners several times.

The Hardys called her Toodie since mother and daughter had the same first name. As mentioned earlier, I also called her Toodie. She was a delight to know, very moral, decent, always happy, very popular, a good dancer, and certainly very pretty. At that time she was an executive secretary at the National American Red Cross headquarters in Washington. All of my family members liked her. A year later we were engaged, and we married on June 8, 1946, at St. Gabriel's Catholic Church in Washington.

While engaged, Toodie told me that if we married, being a stay-at-home wife and mother would be her wish if the Lord were to bless us with a family. She also said that she would continue working until such time as a baby would be due.

I thoroughly enjoyed my civilian engineering position and the wonderful professionals with whom I worked. However, the Army life that I had experienced had given me a quality of discipline and camaraderie that I did not find in the civilian world. Additionally, it had the military potential for travel and career advancement.

In early October 1946 I received an unexpected letter from the Army asking if I would return to active duty as an Engineer Faculty Instructor at the U.S. Army Engineer School at Ft. Belvoir, Virginia. At that time we were living in an apartment building on Georgia Avenue, just across the street from Walter Reed Army General Hospital.

Should I accept the appointment? The commute from our apartment to Ft. Belvoir would be about twenty-five miles each way. The route passed the American Red Cross Headquarters and the Washington National Airport Pentagon Annex where Mrs. Hardy worked. I could take them both to and from work. It also meant the use of the Army Commissary, Post Exchange, Medical Care, and other benefits. The big negative was that I'd have to give up my university night school during the adjustment period, when I would be on duty as officer of the guard, when attending mandatory officers night classes and other related evening/night duties.

Grace had never been exposed to Army life; however, she was anxious to learn. The potential for family overseas travel also greatly interested her.

Ft. Belvoir

After considerable thought and evaluation with Grace, college professors, and family, I elected to accept a stabilized four-year teaching assignment at the Army Engineer School at Ft. Belvoir.

Prior to teaching a single class, all potential instructors had to complete a two-week instructor training course we called "Charm School." Charm School was managed and taught by civilians with Ph.D's in education. To teach any subject, one must first master the topic(s) completely. A bell curve was used to measure the instructors effectiveness, and where appropriate, revise the lesson plans for use of a back-up instructor if needed. This stabilized instructor assignment lasted from 1947 to 1950.

The class of ten included experienced officers in the grades of lieutenant, captain and major. Among the subjects taught and examined were appearance of the uniform, classroom techniques including use of a blackboard pointer, platform assurance, charts, 35mm slides, shoes shined, proper wearing of decorations, class control, and even the Army-style hair cut and shave. They were all fair game for critique.

We began with five-minute introductory talks, then ten-minute, twenty-five, and finally a forty-five minute class presentations. Classmates had to critique each other's platform delivery and subject matter, regardless of rank. As an example, a critique would point out to a potential instructor the number of times the officer said "Ah"or took a long pause.

After joining the Engineering Department, I was assigned to teach mines/demolitions, engineer reconnaissance, rigging, engineer tools, field fortifications, camouflage and water supply. The officer students came from ROTC (Reserve Officer Training Corps), USMA (United States Military Academy-West Point), and the National Guard. There were also other commissioned officers who transferred from various branches of the military and elsewhere to the Army Corp of Engineers. There was also a special engineering course for senior non-commissioned officers (NCO's). Classroom and field training took up some 25 to 30 hours per week for the instructors. Writing and grading tests, individual help to students, and administrative requirements consumed the rest of the work week.

Back to Europe...Austria

In December 1946, Grace and I were living in government quarters on Maiden Lane in Cameron Valley, Virginia near Alexandria.

Our next door neighbor was a civilian employee of the Army at Ft. Belvoir, Virginia. It was at his residence that we first saw a television set. It showed a test pattern in most of the daytime and a children's show called "Howdy Doody" with Buffalo Bob talking to a manikin (dummy). The other program was a weekly Navy series called "Victory at Sea" which depicted the war in the Pacific. The picture itself was five inches in diameter, a gun-type that used vacuum tubes. (Of course it was black and white back then.)

On August 8, 1947, our daughter, Kathleen, was born at Walter Reed General Hospital in Washington. Our second daughter, Suzanne, was born at Walter Reed on the 22nd of August 1948. Our son, Robert, was also born at Walter Reed, on 28 March 1950.

A few months before Robert's birth I received overseas Alert Orders, telling me I was to be assigned to the U.S. Forces, Austria. Six weeks after Robert's birth, our family reported to the New York Military Port of Embarkation for the Austrian assignment. We shipped a new Studebaker car early so as to have a vehicle close to our arrival time at the port of Bremerhaven in occupied Germany.

Grace's dad, Mr. Hardy drove us to the New York Military Port of Embarkation. He stayed with us while being processed. It was rough for him to see us taking our little people away from grandparents.

We were assigned family accommodations aboard the U.S. Army Transport General Patch. The ocean crossing was very smooth. We had a man named Waldo who made our beds, cleaned our cabin, was our table waiter, and took care of us in general.

On our arrival at Bremerhaven, we boarded a train called the Mozart Express. Next stop: Linz, Austria, on the Danube River, which was to be our home for the next four years. Linz was near Salzburg, a city we also enjoyed.

Adolf Hitler was born in Austria. As the Chancellor of Germany, he annexed Austria as part of the Third Reich. Accordingly, at the end of WWII, Austria was divided into four sectors of occupation by the Russians, French, English and the U.S.

Our government quarters address was C-35 Froshburg, on a cul-de-sac with a view of the Danube and the Linz cathedral from the second floor. It had a large, beautiful back yard for the children. Another benefit was that little children about the age of ours lived in the adjacent quarters next door.

I was assigned as the Commanding Officer Company "D" 70th Engineer Combat Battalion at Camp McCauley, formally a German Air Base. Grace had a staff of three Austrians to help her run the house. The houseman, Joseph, fired the furnace in the winter and maintained hot water, washed windows and the car, moved furniture, cut the grass, made repairs and maintained the house. The housemaid, Maria, cooked, cleaned the house, operated the washing machine and ironed clothes. We also had a nursemaid for the children named Renie.

The Army paid for Joseph and Maria, and we paid for Renie. She had her bedroom adjacent to the children's. Joseph and Maria lived with their own families. The three Austrians spoke English as well as German. It did not take long before the children were singing nursery rhymes in German.

We all loved the beauty, culture, and traditions of the Austrian people. Grace quickly adjusted to the role of a young Army wife overseas. The other wives were fond of her and the older officers admired her wit and her nice appearance. She fully enjoyed the use of the Army Commissary, Post Exchange, Military Theater, as well as the companionship of the other Army wives. On her many automobile shopping trips to Munich, Germany with her friend Ruth Thon, Grace would return home with beautiful figurines, cameras, cuckoo clocks, artists' drawings, and many other souvenirs which she enjoyed all her life.

The Camp McCauley Post Exchange in Austria had a great selection of children's toys. I noticed a pedal car that could be made to look exactly like a jeep for a little three-year old boy. My mechanics noticed my purchase and asked if they could put some of our decals on the little vehicle. When they returned it, I was truly surprised. It had been painted Army Green with my USA vehicle number and white star markings. The front bumper said "Captain Robert, D-6, 70th Engineers" in white letters.

The jeep rear had a salvaged bed spring with welding rod attached and secured to the frame. When driven, this "antenna" moved like it was from an operating radio unit. It had a windshield that would lay flat on the hood, like a tactical vehicle. It even had a salvaged rug serving as a floor mat. That jeep returned to the USA with us along with the household furniture. It was driven until all of the rubber on the tires was worn away, and even later Robert would drive it on the rims.

Company "D" 70th Engineer Combat Battalion had been a separate National Guard engineer company. When it was federalized, it was ordered to Austria and became an organic company of the then under strength 70th Engineers.

There was a number of "good old boy" civilians-at-heart soldiers in Company "D." For instance, their officers did not attend reveille. Nor was their first sergeant up to my standards. My first order as CO was that all company officers and enlisted personnel would stand reveille with the new first sergeant that transferred to my command. His name was "Two-Gun" Foster. We took reveille together six days a week. Then things began to fall into place quickly.

Company "D" had been assigned a highly classified mission. Because of the nature of the mission, I required that every man would be a qualified demolition soldier. That included my mechanics, cooks, and clerical personnel. I had my training officer schedule demolition training at night. When it rained or snowed, we fired explosives. It was about this time that I was promoted to the grade of captain.

During the Cold War, the Danube River at Linz separated the Austrian Soviet Zone from the U.S. Austrian Zone. The Commanding Officer "D" Company had a written classified order directing me to blow the six-lane Linz Bridge should the Russians be about to make an unmistakable overt act to cross the bridge.

Like any bridge, there were certain critical points at specific locations that, if subjected to demolition charges, will result in bridge failure. Each of my demolition teams was assigned to their individual designated demolition points. Cooks, clerks, and mechanics were trained as back up or replacement demotion personnel if needed.

Explosive charges for each designated demolition point were maintained truck-loaded, charges calculated, pre-measured non-electrical and electric firing wire (for dual firing), blasting caps, blasting machines, and galvanometers were pre-loaded.

Unlike Checkpoint Charlie in Berlin, where U.S. and Russian MPs with their tanks and cannons pointed at each other, the Linz bridge was totally open and unguarded. I selected the most critical bridge point as my command post, and charged all of my officers and senior NCOs with the demolition of their previously assigned targets.

At that time, Austria was known as the "spy capital" of the Cold War in Europe. We had to be aware of Soviet spies and Austrian paid agents in our zone. The Russians had electronic equipment in vehicles that could enabled them, or certain Austrians, to monitor classified conversations unless counter measures were employed.

Even simple ones, such as whenever we would study the plan and address such matters as explosive requirements, radio communications, river currents, backup demolition company soldier assets, potential civilian interference, dependent evacuation, and Soviet spy activities, we would have a commercial radio station on with the volume louder than our speech.

Each "D" Company truck was tailor-loaded for its TNT (trinitrotoluene) particular bridge target along with electrical firing wire, as well as time fuse for non-electric firing. There was no authority to pre-load the trucks with these heavy stagnant loads. I requested my commander, Lt. Col. Clock, to concur in my written request through military channels to the Army headquarters in Austria for an exception to regulations so that everything required for operation could be permanently pre-loaded.

There would be no time to load thousands of pounds of explosives and equipment should the mission become active. Our unit developed an unusual truck stand for each vehicle that took the weight off of the springs while in modified storage mode. It permitted the operator to drive off the stand and then let the truck springs take the load in the normal manner.

Our tactical support was the 510th Field Artillery Battalion, which would give us 105mm indirect firing from their cannons. The 4th Armored Reconnaissance Battalion, with their M-24 General Chaffee light tanks, would provide tank versus tank fire.

Dependents were required to maintain their vehicles with at least one full five-gallon container of auto fuel. They also were requested to have water and long shelf-life food, e.g., canned sardines, saltine crackers, cookies, peanut butter, and dried powdered milk, along with plastic eating utensils in the vehicle trunk with flashlights. Blankets, paper plates, toilet paper, and extra clothing were also recommended. This was an individual family responsibility.

Headquarters 70th Engineers with its Headquarters/ Service and line Companies "A," "B," and "C" were stationed about 100 miles south of "D" Company. They were all in the mountain pass areas bellow Salzburg. Their mission, with an infantry regiment, was to deny the Russian access to command and logistic facilities in Italy.

There was only one direct two-lane asphalt road from Linz to Salzburg. Almost anywhere along the evacuation route, saboteurs could position farm equipment or vehicles to block the escape of American dependents. For that reason, many wives had weapons where they could demand that local anti-U.S. individuals remove such road blocks. I had such a weapon and wanted to train Grace in its use for her protection and that of our children. She didn't like guns and refused that option, telling me that would never take place. She was correct, thank God.

My Combat Engineer Company appeared only once in the initial operational classified orders. I'm sure because there would not be enough survivors of the bridge destruction mission to be tasked for subsequent combat missions. We were certainly a rear guard unit. A rear guard unit is, for the most part, frequently sacrificed to save other units, or to hold on until other or larger friendly forces could be committed to the fight. "D" Company had no anti-tank weapons except for the 3.5" rocket launcher (bazooka). We also had 30- and 50-caliber machine guns, and M-1 rifles, 30-caliber carbines, and a few pistols and, of course, lots of explosives.

The Russians that were expected to oppose us during our bridge demolition operation, was always on my mind. I knew that the 3.5" bazookas had the capacity to immobilize tanks if our two-man teams were expert shots, and hit the Russian tanks in the tracks or drive wheel mechanisms. I wanted them to stop those tanks hundreds of yards in front of my guys. All combat units were sent to weapons ranges in Germany for live firing of artillery, tank weapons, infantry arms, and demolition firing. While there, I wanted my soldiers to gain personal confidence in the 3.5" rocket launcher. I obtained a number of 2x4 wooden posts and had them placed upright at different distances: 150 and 200 yards. I said any crew who could hit the 2x4s beyond the maximum operational range would be given a three-day pass.

Very quickly they destroyed the targets at 150 and 200 yards. When they moved to greater distances, they blew away those posts as well. There were so many crews destroying posts at the maximum range that I had to stop giving away the three-day pass business, otherwise I would soon have everybody on pass. It was very reassuring to me to see the confidence that this training attained. Some of the crews said "bring 'em on." Thank God, we were never put to that test.

Due to my classified operational mission in Austria, only a very few men could be granted a three-day pass. One such pass meant that three other men could only have a one-day pass. Accordingly, I granted three-day passes sparingly. One day, my first sergeant, "Two-Gun" Foster told me that one of our soldiers wanted permission to talk to me. He had already asked his sergeant and lieutenant for permission, as was required, to talk with me.

I asked "Two-Gun" if he knew what was on the soldier's mind. He said the man would request a three-day pass to go to Vienna. I said that he had better have a good reason. The man came in, saluted me, stood at strict attention, and said he had gone through channels and had permission to talk to me. I then asked him the nature of his visit. His uniform was pressed, he sported a new hair cut, and he had shaved so close that he had no sign of a beard at all. He said that if I would grant him that pass he would return on time. He was an excellent soldier. After thinking about his request, I decided to grant his pass request with this remark. "If you do not return within three days, never come back!" He had the last two words. "Yes sir!" Then he saluted, did an about face. The next morning he departed for Vienna .

As earlier stated every officer and enlisted man was required to stand reveille six days a week in the fatigue work uniform. On the third day of the pass in question, there was that soldier in the rear dressed in his class "A" (dress) uniform. After the formation was dismissed, "Two-Gun" Foster entered my office and announced that the three-day pass soldier had obtained permission to speak with me again. I asked the sergeant what it was he wanted to speak to me about. Sergeant Foster said that he wanted another three-day pass. I told my sergeant that he'd better have the best reason that I have ever heard, and I had heard a lot from experts!

The soldier knocked on the door, came in, and saluted. I noted that he looked a little worn around the edges. I asked him to state his business. He said that he needed to return to Vienna. There was a policy that commanding officers had the discretion to grant leave or passes in excess of general policy, based on compassionate reasons.

He knew about that policy. I asked him to state his business for such a request. He looked me in the eye and said, "Sir, based on those passionate reasons."

Two-Gun and I tried not to laugh as I thought about what he said. The room was very quiet. I knew that he was truthfully asking permission based on the "compassionate reason" requirement, but because he is so nervous he had said, "passionate reasons." We were looking into each other's the eyes, and I said "Go back to Vienna but be back in three days!" And three days later, he was back on time.

In any large organization, most personnel contribute to the company or to the team's mission. As the young twenty-seven-year-old "D" Company commander, it was my experience that 99.9 % of my men were good troops. I did however have one problem soldier. He was an alcoholic; a private first class named Meheen. He was a good soldier until payday. Then he would go to town, get drunk, and not return for several reveilles. When he finally sobered up, he would come back AWOL (Absent Without Leave).

All of the soldiers were observing how I would handle such an infraction as I well knew. The initial punishment would be extra duty at the end of each day for a week or so, depending on the number of days the soldier was AWOL. The next occurrence, I reduced him to the grade of buck private. And the third time he was court martialed. Before each punishment I would explain to him that I had an obligation to maintain discipline and order. Each time he said he was sorry.

After the last AWOL, I had taken a step to keep him from getting a drink from his whisky hiding places. Every day, I had the motor pool sergeant march him to the parts and tool building where he worked. Once inside, the man could not exit since he would have to pass directly in front of the sergeant. One day I received an unexpected visit from the Inspector General. He told me that private Meheen had a complaint against me. He wanted to see Meheen now and I was to accompany him. We went to the motor pool building, and I told the sergeant to have Meheen come out to see the IG.

We waited and waited The sergeant said, "Sir, I personally put him in the parts and tool room. He never got past me, but he's not there."

Now the parts room was heated in winter with a wood stove. This was August. We heard a strange sound, looked up into the huge stove pipe, and there was Meheen stuck in the pipe, and drunk. He had stashed extra whisky in the tool room. With that, I said to the IG, "Here is your poor persecuted soldier." At that he shook his head and departed.

While stationed at Camp McCauley, I knew a number of Army civilian employees. One of them was a man named "Melvin." He worked in the local ordnance office in some sort of administrative position. One day he telephoned me and asked to meet me in private. That seemed a bit unusual but I agreed to the time and place for the meeting. When I arrived he said that he already had spoken with my Battalion Commander (Lt. Colonel Clock) and had his permission for the meeting.

He said that his ordinance job was not the only reason that he was in Austria. He said that a number of Hungarians had attempted to escape the Soviet control of Hungary which shared a border with Austria. He once spoke of it as the Austro-Hungarian Empire, as the two had once been one country. Melvin said that he had paid a farmer on the border to bring one of the Soviet anti-personnel (A.P.) mines in one of his fields, as evidence of the mines having been installed along the entire border as a barrier against Hungarians escaping Soviet domination. Many people had been killed and many others had lost limbs setting off such mines in their attempt for freedom.

Melvin said that he knew of my demolition, mine and booby trap experience, and that I was considered the most highly qualified in the entire command for the task of determining the steps and procedures to neutralize those devices. I was not sure that he was an agent so I told him that I would call Colonel Clock to insure that he knew what I had been asked to do.

When I got back from the meeting, I immediately telephoned Colonel Clock, and he told me that Melvin had talked with him, and that headquarters in Salzburg knew of the mission. He also said that it was my choice to either decline or accept. Should I decline it would not hurt my career since it was outside of my duties as a commander of troops. I asked him if the mission went badly – that is, if I was blown up in the attempt to neutralize the device – would the Army (or U.S. government) provide financial support to my family. He responded in the affirmative.

The next night at an empty building, Melvin introduced me to a big Austrian who was wearing traditional lederhosen (short leather pants). He had a big suit case, and when opened, it was full of dirt and one of the anti-personnel mines.

I questioned him as to the depth it had been buried, the distance from the other mines, the minefield pattern, how long it had been buried, and other related questions.

He then departed, and I was never to see him again. Then Melvin prepared to leave. He pointed to a telephone and asked me to call him after I had neutralized the mine. Before each planned action or procedure, I would write what I intended to do. After that worked, I would plan and write the next step.

Finally, I was successful in determining the procedure to safely neutralize the mine. I telephoned him. He asked me to make a sketch of the device and write the steps and procedures to be taken to render the anti-personnel mine harmless. On completion of the sketches and hand-written notes, I telephoned Melvin to pick up his new "toy." He said that everything would be translated into German.

After that night, I never spoke with Melvin or Colonel Clock about what I had done. I hope what I did saved some lives and limbs, and had enabled some people to escape to freedom in the West. Thank God, I was able to very carefully study it, and with a paint brush, a safety wire, and my hands, successfully neutralized the anti-personnel mine.

Happy New Year's Eve

The commanding general was a three-star general, "Bull" Kendal. It was customary at Army facilities on New Year's Eve that officers dressed in formal uniforms with medals displayed, patent leather shoes, and their ladies appeared in evening gowns with corsages. There was orchestra music and presentation of the Colors. Every New Year's the same routine took place at the NCO Club and the Soldiers' Club.

At exactly midnight, as 1946 became 1947, General Kendal ordered the tactical troops to move out immediately and proceed to their firing positions or demolition target assembly areas. All the male personnel departed the various clubs, leaving their wives to get home as best they could.

Not all the soldiers were fit for duty. As an example, a tank crew normally driven by a corporal who was too full of beer or whisky meant that a sergeant had to take over the driver's duties. And in some case, a lieutenant might be in the gunner's station. The same occurred with an artillery gun crew. We combat engineers arrived promptly on target. A specific bridge target might have a squad sergeant in charge of several squads.

We spent the following three days in the deep Austrian snow, on our targets, wearing dress shoes and our best uniforms. The exercise terminated on the third day with every body having beards, wet feet, and looking very unruly in their finest military attire. On that third day, the soldiers were dismissed.

Officers and NCOs were ordered to the theater. The general said from the stage that he knew all hands were asking among themselves, why did the general do this? He explained that if the Soviets were to attack, it would not likely occur in the pleasant months of May and June. Nor would it take place in the early afternoon. He went on to say that he knew there would be certain officers unable to function properly, due to the degree of their celebrating on New Year's Eve, especially before midnight. He said the same problems applied at the NCO and Soldiers' clubs. He then congratulated all the personnel, since everybody had made it on target, and those who had arrived "under the weather" would quickly recover enough to take over their regular duties.

He added that the exercise also gave some subordinates the self-assurance to know that they could step into their bosses' jobs in an emergency. A very good lesson for all. That's the type of the Soldier Army that I was proud to serve. Tough and battle ready.

Kitchen Confession

Every company sized troop unit in Austria subscribed to numerous U.S. magazines like *Time, Life, Look, Reader's Digest,* and sports and car magazines. (No *Playboy.*) Each week, the company clerk would place the newly received publications in the recreation Day Room and trash the older editions.

One Saturday after troop inspection, I was introduced to an interesting and gentle old Catholic priest name Father Valentine, who was an English teacher in a local boys boarding high school. During our conversation he noticed the company clerk trashing the outdated issues and replacing them with the news ones He asked me if he could take those being thrown away and use them as class teaching aids. I replied of course and that in the future I would have the out-dated issues save for me and that I would then deliver a bundle to the school.

After three or four weeks, I took the initial out-dated magazines to Fr. Valentine. He was delighted and gave me a tour of the school, including their kitchen, where there were four somewhat overweight and jolly Austrian lady cooks preparing a meal in institutional size pots, producing a wonderful fragrance of old world foods. None of them spoke or understood any English.

After several hundred years of cooks, priests and students walking and compacting the earthen kicthen floor, it looked, felt, and had the character of concrete. On one of my later visits, Fr. Valentine suggested we revisit the kitchen. While sitting there, he brought me some local cheese, bread, crackers and Lizner beer. What a treat.

Such wonderful snacks in the kitchen together with the great kitchen smells made for an unforgettable afternoon. Father Valentine and I became great friends as between bites, we discusses various economic, political, social, and historical events.

Fr. Valentine knew from our talks together that I was Roman Catholic, and that I always attended Mass on Sundays with my family. And as was my custom, I did my confession before Mass.

On this particular magazine delivery Saturday, Fr. Valentine asked if I would like to go to Confession before cheese and beer. Of course, I said, that would save time for me the next day. I knelt on the floor next to Fr. Valentine's chair. I made my confession to God as he held my hands. All the while, the cooks were talking, machines were washing and slicing the potatoes, and they were carrying on with their other ancillary kitchen activities. The cooks went about their duties as if we were not there in the kitchen. I felt very close to God in this wholesome environment. It was my first confession in the kitchen, but not the last.

A Bad Apple

During the conclusion of a three-day planned field training exercise, just as I walked into my quarters, there was a telephone call from one-star Brigadier General (BG) Marsden, the local base commander, about an officer who had threatened to shoot his wife. The officer was known to drink heavily and had been barred from the area where his wife lived. Due to drinking off duty and his wife's alleged beatings by her husband, separate quarters in different cities had been assigned. The general had a report that this officer, Lieutenant George B was likely already in the wife's quarters.

I reminded the CG that George B had been one of my company officers, and that I had found him unfit for the special assignment of my unit. Additionally, I told the general that after three days in the deep snow with little sleep, eating cold field rations, and insuring that all military personnel and their equipment and weapons were properly secured at the termination of the training, I was not in the best of moods. I added that if the lieutenant gave me any trouble, I'd shoot him. At that the general said that he was sending a black-'n-white Military Police (MP) car. The MPs would be armed but I was not, repeat, not to be armed.

In a few minutes, two armed MPs arrived and we were off to Linz. On arrival at his front door, I stationed an MP on each side of the door so as not to be in his view. When George opened the door, he had a drink in his hand. He expressed surprise to see me. When I entered the apartment I saw two hand guns on the coffee table located behind him. I wanted a reason to get the weapons, remove the ammunition, and search for his wife to see if she was in need of immediate medical attention...or worse.

That was now my first priority. I said to George, "As a gentleman, you could offer me a drink." When he went to the kitchen to fix my drink, I unloaded both weapons and let in the two MPs. When George returned with the drink, I informed him that he was under arrest, and then we searched his apartment. Fortunately, the only person there was George. He offered an excuse blaming his wife for the problems. I told George that I had no interest in his martial issues. George then asked me if I would grant him a few minutes to talk with his wife on the phone from his bedroom. I told him, "Yes, but make it short."

I waited a few minutes and then heard a Porsche sports car race out of the parking lot below. I knew it was George. Immediately I went into his bedroom There I saw the window open, and looking outside, I noticed the heavy duty European-type iron rain spout that he must have used to escape arrest.

I immediately realized that I should not have permitted him to "call his wife." I summoned the MPs and told them that he'd escaped, and that we would try to catch him. We piled into the MP vehicle with lights and siren on. I then radioed the MPs station in Wels telling them to go to the hotel where his wife lived and report to me if his Porsche showed up. A few minutes later they radioed back that his car was parked in front of the hotel bar. I told them to guard that car and not permit anyone to use it, and detain anyone asking why they could not use the car. We arrived a few minutes later.

When I entered the bar and saw George and his wife arm in arm with drinks, talking cheerfully, I said, "George, you are still under arrest and this MP will cuff you and put you in the police car."

Then his wife turned to me and said, "Captain Ramos, you never liked my George."

I knew in that moment that she was the person who had initiated the entire episode. I also knew that she was as nutty as he. So at that I told the MP to put her in the car, too, and we would take both of them to the Camp McCauley Military Hospital where a doctor had been alerted to expect us.

End of the story? No. Years later while in Philadelphia on National Guard Duty, I saw on the front page of the *Philadelphia Enquire* newspaper a report that George had shot a young woman in the Fort Belvoir Officers Club. He told her that she could not date any other officers but him. She objected, and he shot her in the breast and took off with the law in hot pursuit. As I remember, she survived and he went to the federal prison at Ft. Leavenworth, Kansas. So much for MP duty.

Specialized Engineer Training

The Commanding General Tactical Command Austria, Brigadier General Fry, determined that the requirements for demolition operations exceeded the capabilities of his modest assigned engineer force. Since I had extensive WWII experience, and had taught that subject for four years at the U.S. Army Engineer School at Ft. Belvoir, I was ordered to organize, equip, and train non-engineer troops in demolitions. Personnel trained included infantry, artillery, and tankers. Among the elements I introduced were training procedures to eliminate time fuse misfires. My program was later adopted by the Army. Hundreds of soldiers completed the training.

Military personnel who attended the demolition school were asked by their commanders if the time and experience provided them with the confidence to undertake mine and demolition missions if there were no engineer troops available. Apparently all soldiers responded in the affirmative.

Fog and Ordnance

There was an all-glass green house on our Camp McCauley base in Linz. One day the moisture concentrations was extremely high due to a heavy fog. Since training was paramount, we fired charges regardless of the weather. On this day, the heavy air and the vibrations caused by the explosions of the ordnance had a deleterious effect on the glass house.

All of a sudden a Military Police Jeep arrived, with a soldier asking who is in charge. I said, "I am." The MP told me that General Marsden wanted me to report to his office ASAP.

Shortly after I arrived at the CG's office, he invited me to sit, and he told me that the "former" green house no longer had any glass panels. As he spoke, I wondered how many years it would take me to pay for all that glass.

But General Marsden said, "What happened in the training this morning reminded me of a somewhat smaller green house I destroyed many years ago as a young captain." He went on to instruct me that during the heavy fog conditions, I needed to reschedule our live firing training for a more favorable day. I had the last two words – "Yes sir!" – and I departed for the demolition class again.

The Heart and Soul of an Army

Shortly after that assignment, General Fry ordered me to activate, organize, select cadre, and classroom and staff living facilities for a Tactical Command Non-commissioned Officers Academy. My battalion commander told the general that he needed me for an assignment in the Salzburg mountain area. General Fry told Lieutenant Colonel Clock that I was needed for his assignment since the results would benefit the entire command, not just a single company.

I was not present or consulted about this, of course. And I had issues on the home front. Since the Soviet Army was on the other side of the Danube River from Linz, at the town of Urfahr, many military wives, especially those with children, preferred living in Salzburg and more southern areas towards Italy, rather than being in Linz and so close to the Russians. But the Ramos family loved the quarters we had in Linz; also, our military friends were there.

The proximity of the Soviet troops did not bother Grace. She had said to me on many occasions that even if I was transferred away from Linz that she and the children would remain in our quarters in Linz on the Danube. She loved the area, and she was fortunate to have trusted and dedicated help for baby Robert, along with the nurse maid, Renie, the house frau, Maria, and Joseph, the house man.

The classes and troops living areas of the NCO Academy at Camp McCauley had beautiful but neglected wood floors. I wanted this Academy to be spit and polish. Since no commercial wood polish was available after the war, we used shoe polish with wonderful results. This is but one example of many problems to be resolved. I was designated as the School Commandant. All objectives were attained and the work met with official kudos.

New Brothers in Arms

My final assignment was the training of an Austrian Government hand-picked police cadre of former senior Austrian army officers. These officers were destined to be leaders of the reconstituted Austrian army. Its commander was a Colonel Prysil who formerly was a lieutenant general in the combined German-Austrian Army of WWII. Like Germany, after the war Austria was occupied by the Allies, and under the terms of the surrender agreement, neither country could have an army for some time. Also, when the occupation was to end, all four powers would leave Austria at the same time.

The U.S. government knew that the Soviets were in the process of military training and equipping their satellite countries. This work that I was doing was then classified. U.S. equipment and weapons were shipped to this location for joint training. After the work day, I would eat in the mess with the men I was training, and over time I learned that some of these officers had been in Normandy on D-day. Recognizing our new situation, we would shake hands, have a bottle of Linzer Beer, and acknowledge that we were now brothers in arms and glad that each one of us survived the war. I was able to return to my Linz quarters on weekends only.

Star of David

During an extensive vacation during occupation duty in Austria, I visited, Hitler's "Eagles Nest" in Germany on the border with Austria, high up in a beautiful mountain area. When I entered the Grand Room, I was drawn to the largest fireplace that I had ever seen. My memory tells me it was about twenty feet wide with a very beautiful wood mantle piece.

On that mantle piece, I could not miss an inscription from an American Jewish paratrooper of the 101st Airborne Division, who had taken his bayonest or another sharp tool and had carved the Star of David, his name, "New York," and the date in it.

This was about 1952. Many years later, in 1992, during a return visit to Normandy and Hitler's Eagles Nest, I noticed a different mantle piece above the fireplace. No more soldier's Star of David. I presumed that the locale people wanted to forget all about Hitler and the massive destruction of the Jewish people, along with Austria's participation in World War II.

The Ramos Family Returns to the USA

The family was flying home on a conventional four engine Lockheed Constellation military aircraft – commercial jet airliners were not yet in service – and we were over the ocean at night, when one engine became non-operational. From the flight deck, an announcement was made telling the military and their dependents that the aircraft could fly all night on three engines without any problem. However, we were directed to put on our emergency survival vests.

The aircraft crew assigned a non-accompanied soldier to each child where the parents had more than two children. Grace had baby Rosemary, I was responsible for Robert, and two soldiers had Kathy and Sue. Should a second engine quit we would have made a water landing. Grace said, "No worry, the blessed Virgin Mary knows our situation. We will arrive safely." What an example of faith!

We landed the next morning at Dover, Delaware, and were delighted to see Grace's parents waiting at the gate to welcome us home. When we arrived from Austria, our daughter, Kathleen, was almost six, Suzanne was not yet five, and Robert was just three years old. They had heard of their grandparents but now three years later, they were strangers to the children.

From their experience, the children related to all senior citizens as being Austrians, who would be speaking German to them. Mr. and Mrs. Hardy were trying to kiss and hug everybody at once. As Mrs. Hardy picked him up, Robert said to his mother, "I don't like this new haus frau and this new haus master ."

Our newest daughter, Rosemary, was a baby in Grace's arms. She had decided not to tell anyone in the States about her pregnancy, to preclude her parents worrying about her. Our three older children loved their new blonde baby sister. They called her "Row." The children spoke German, sang nursery rhymes in German, and spoke to

Grace and me in English.

I was assigned to support the Pennsylvania National Guard's Engineer Battalions, primarily in the Philadelphia area, but there were no Army quarters or any other Army support available to me. That meant that I had to begin searching for a home that we could afford and that would satisfy our family's needs. I was authorized 30 days leave to find a place to live and organize for Guard Duty. Grace and the children stayed with her parents at their home in Tacoma Park, Maryland, until I could find a house that Grace said would serve everyone well.

I purchased a new Plymouth Station Wagon and headed for Philadelphia. I remembered my buddy Lt. Mike Cosella who lived in Philadelphia and was a Combat Brother WW11 Officer in the 254th Engineers. Mike had recovered from his war injuries, and returned to work for the Pennsylvania Railroad as an official. When I telephoned Mike's home his wife Kay said that Mike had mentioned my name in letters to her several times. She gave me Mike's office phone and said to call him right away and plan to be their dinner guest that evening. Much of the dinner conversation that night was about real estate at a reasonable distance from the two military armories and our WW11 "old days."

Mike and Kay had no children and a bedroom which was never used. They insisted that I use it until I had my own place and then the family could join me. I was happy to find a three-bedroom house in the suburb of Roslyn which was near a Catholic School, a Catholic church, and great neighbors, which was a reasonable commute to the armories. What we all missed was Marie the maid, Joseph the haus master and Renie the children's adopted true friend. Once we were reunited as a family again, Grace assumed the typical role as a mom and homemaker.

My relationship with the Pennsylvania National Guard's commanding officers was initially professional, and later evolved into a very cordial and long term relationship. The commanding officers were Lt. Col. Jack Betson of the103rd and Lt. Col. Bill Britton of the 644th, both Engineer Combat Battalions. In addition to my official National Guard duties, I undertook a recruiting mission of returning former national guard officers to active Guard duty. One of them was Lt. Mike Cosella, who became "Uncle Mike" and his wife "Aunt Kay" to our children. One of my favorite photos is the Davy Crockett outfits purchased for the children by the Cosella's. Mike died of cancer in 1962.

(This historical note...National Guard Soldiers have been known as Volunteers, Militate, Minute Men, and in recent history as National Guardsman.)

Except for the two week summer camp field training, Guard soldiers trained one evening each week at the local armory. They wore the uniform only in the armory. The Federal government funded the armory drill pay, uniforms, weapons, vehicles, and training needs like ammunition, bridging, medical and other training equipment. There was a requirement that an officer from the Regular Army certified that the training and federal monies expended made the Guard organizations immediately available for integration into the federal Army in times of war or national emergencies.

While in this assignment I was promoted to the grade of major. My duties included three guard battalions and several separate guard companies. This meant lots of regular day work, plus many night drills, and summer two week camp sessions. My office consisted of myself, and one regular army NCO, SFC Alva Smith, who had been a four-year war prisoner of the Japanese, and a survivor of the Bataan Death march.

National Summer Training

In August of 1985 a severe flood occurred in Stroudsburg, Pennsylvania. Flood waters washed away or severely damaged bridges, roads leaving debris, pregnant women in deed of hospital transportation, dead bodies and major culverts destroyed. At that time the 103rd Engineer Combat Battalion was conducting their Annual Summer Field Training in the nearby Indiantown Gap Military Reservation.

The governor ordered them to proceed to Stroudsburg to relieve the suffering, and to help in restoring infrastructure. As the regular Army Instructor, I, along with Sergeant Smith, accompanied the battalion on this mission.

The 103rd Engineers constructed a 200-foot steel panel Bailey bridge, reinforced other damaged bridges, rescued stranded civilians, operated portable water locations, and provided other urgently needed support.

Advanced Education Requirement for Higher Command

The regular Army had a series of schools for the post-graduate education of their officers. In addition to officers from the other branches – the Marines, Air Force and Navy – there were also officers from friendly foreign governments, the FBI, Department of State, and other nominated senior civilian officials who could attend these higher education institutions. Within the Army, competition for enrollment was very competitive. Prospective attendees were selected not by request or application but from the different career branches in the Pentagon.

While on my stabilized assignment with the National Guard, orders were received reassigning me as a student to attend the Command and General Staff College (CGSC) at Ft. Leavenworth, Kansas. Selection is based on many factors including efficiency reports, troop duty, training of reserve forces, promotion potential and other specialties. I was one of a few engineer branch officers selected. Its primary mission was the training of officers with demonstrated capability for higher command at the Division, Corps, and Field Army levels.

After Command and General Staff College, certain assignments had a prerequisite that an officer under consideration for specific Command, Diplomatic, or General Staff assignment must be a graduate of the Command General Staff College. We studied in great detail logistics, nuclear weapons, interaction with civilian government officials, the press, critical civilian utilities and active power generation plants, numbers and location of national petroleum manufacturing facilities, and other critical defense issues. All classmates were dedicated students except for one foreign general. He was the son of the Dominican Republic Dictator Trujillo who had been made a general at a very young age.

He signed in at the CGSC and immediately departed for Hollywood. We never saw him. He made Hollywood his "college." The press featured reports on him buying lavish gifts for so-called Hollywood sirens. Obviously he did not graduate, at least not from CGSC.

In later years I served as the Command Engineer with former non-engineer classmates of the CGSC in Korea, at Ft. Benning, Georgia, and in the Dominican Revolution with the Inter-American Peace Force. At graduation I was assigned as the Operation Officer of the 13th Engineer Combat Battalion, 7th Infantry Division, Korea. In 1956, as a graduate of the Command General Staff College, I was later assigned as the Inter-American Peace Force (IAPF) Command Engineer during the Dominican Revolution of 1965-1966.

As I recall, Korea at that time was a 12- or 18-month assignment. Grace decided to remain in Roslyn with the children since they were doing so well in school, and they had wonderful neighbors. Plus, Grace preferred being in her own home as opposed to living with her parents or with the Ramos family. I certainly couldn't blame her.

It was a tradition when the children were in the primary grades for Grace an I to lead them in saying the Rosary every evening just before they would go to bed. At that time, there were four children. The fifth child, Grace Marie, had not as yet joined the family. Each one of the children would say a decade of ten Hail Mary's with the follow on prayers. As the children became older, that same ritual was followed until higher education pursuant or work caused them to leave the home. Those were very special times in my memory and never to be forgotten.

On the Road Again

Korea Land of the Morning Calm

With orders assigning me to the 13th Engineer Combat Battalion of the 7th Infantry Division in Korea, the mode of transportation from Japan to Korea was the U.S. Air Force Globe Master double-deck troop aircraft. En route, the pilot walked through the huge passenger compartment and noticed me sitting on the canvas bucket seat. He came over to my location, and said, "Hi, classmate."

Sure enough, we had been students at the Command and General Staff College. He told me to follow him up to the flight deck where real seats were available for the crew. He said, "Ray, from the flight deck you can more fully appreciate the Kimpo Airfield approach."

At touchdown and roll out, I could see the war devastation of the structures, and bullet fragments everywhere. A totally dead place. Thank God the shooting had stopped and negotiations had been in process. Previously, a similar aircraft had crashed during the landing procedure, and, as I remembered, all the people on board had perished. After that very unfortunate event, we Army guys called those aircraft the Crash Masters.

After being processed at 7th Division Headquarters, I was taken to report for duty with Lt. Col. Dan Raymond, the Division Engineer who commanded the 13th Engineer Combat Battalion. Dan said, "I've been waiting for your arrival. You will be my S-3 Operations Officer."

Let me explain the "S" designations. S-1 denotes Personnel, S-2 Intelligence, S-3 Operations/Training, and S-4 Supply. Most officers sought the Operations and Training functioning.

As mentioned earlier, the shooting war was over and the Army was in a mode to improve temporary quarters for U.S. and Korean soldiers serving in the 7th Division, before the freezing weather arrived. The earthen roads were dusty when dry, and muddy when wet. Portable hot water showers were much appreciated. Lights and potbelly stoves for heating in winter were installed with engineer soldiers providing technical fire safety and other support.

Another high priority was the construction of a medical dispensary. This was begun in the frigid dead of winter. We used air compressors powering heavy jack hammers to dig thru frozen earth three feet in depth for the footings or trenches. The footings contained frozen water ice crystals that resembled grains of white rice. When we made concrete, the water had to get to boil, and heat the aggregate before we imbedded the iron hold-downs. Once the mix was in place we ignited diesel-fueled smudge pots placed on top of the concrete footings to preclude the concrete from freezing. Covering the smoke-contained footings with corrugated iron roofing sheets for three days permitted the concrete to cure. Then we were able to begin construction. When completed, this facility was a real improvement in the delivery of medical care.

With the cession of hostilities, we began improving the water channel flow under a key bridge span that led to the Division Ammunition Supply Point (ASP). For safety concerns, ammo for rifles, pistols, machine guns, mortar, artillery and other critical supplies/components were stored there, well away from troops, as were other logistical items and division headquarters. The engineer battalion did not select the site.

Korea has a very dry season without any rain but when the rains do come, dry streams become rivers in a short time. I was always concerned that if the North Koreans resumed fighting during the rainy season, and at the same time the raging water under our main bridge to the ASP was damaged or washed away, we could never provide bridging in time to satisfy the division's ammo needs.

The rainy season was now in full swing. Accordingly, I would daily monitor the water level under the bridge. After days of continuous heavy rains, the water was approaching the underside of the bridge. The condition could be critical in a matter of hours. At that point, I commandeered two 60-ton tanks. One was placed over on the far shore abutment, the other on the near shore abutment.

At this time the water was beginning to approach the underside of the stringers. I used the two tanks' combined weight to further anchor the bridge should the rising water come in contact with the bridge underpinnings. Sufficient water pressure pushing against the horizontal street stringers that extended from short to shore could cause the bridge to faile and wash downstream.

A very slight vibration was noted. I knew that if the water continued pushing the span, soon there would be no bridge. We needed a miracle since I could begin mentally to compute the cost to replace the bridge and two Army tanks! As luck would have it, the water flow had reached its peak and was stabilized. After awhile it began to slowly recede and the crisis was over.

A Devout Division Commander

With the cessation of hostilities, the division of some 15,000 personnel had been relocated. The various commanders had initiated some basic work, like general site selection, to have a division chapel honoring the U.S. and South Korean soldiers who lost their lives in fighting with the North Korean and Chinese armies. While this was a noble and appropriate objective, the previous division engineer and his S-3 had reminded the general that such a project had not been approved nor funded.

The response from the general was something like, "I don't want to hear why you can't do it; find a way to do it."

When my new boss arrived, the construction process was already underway. We had approval for a medical facility and troop billets, road improvement, and similar projects. They all came with portland cement allocations. We would conserve just enough cement from approved projects to build the chapel using Korean stone.

The engineers were responsible for the design, materials, construction, and safety of the chapel. However, for the chapel to be cleaned after construction was completed, a prior agreement was made with the headquarters commandant CO for the division band – the clerks, communications technicians, and others; not the engineers – to perform the necessary clean-up tasks, which included removing all construction debris, dusting the pews, washing the windows, washing, waxing, and polishing the floor, and making the chapel look great for the dedication. When the rest of the work was completed, the headquarters commandant personnel reported that they had cleaned the chapel.

Well, before the dedication date, General Sands inspected the chapel to insure that the division headquarters soldiers had cleaned the chapel to comply with his standards and expectations. He discovered that the place was a complete disaster.

General Sands had invited every general officer in the Pacific area to attend the dedication with their spouse. Many had been classmates at West Point many years ago. Korean Generals and wives and other VIPs had also accepted invitations.

The headquarters staff used buckets, mops, hot water and soap, but they had never changed the water. With the mops, they just spread the dirty water and made terrible streaks. Sands was furious. He called my boss Lt. Col. Raymond (later Major General Raymond) and told him to get Ramos and his engineers to the chapel to correct the disgusting mess left by the headquarters staff. I reminded Dan that our engineer soldiers construct and build, but they don't wash windows, wax floors or do any house cleaning. Dan knew that as well as I.

He said to me, "Ray we make a good team. The general is in a spot. His headquarters staff let him down. Pick your people, wax the floors, and wash the windows for me. Do whatever it takes."

I had empathy for our soldiers who had worked so faithfully and now deserved some time off. I said I'd do it, of course, but I hated to tell the men of "C" company who worked to bring the chapel on line that they had to be the maids to clean it up, too.

I almost never went to the so-called Division Officers Club because every senior officer would ask a favor. "Ray, can you send me a load of crushed rock to improve my headquarters." "Ray, could you send me a load of cement to do a special project." I knew the routine and had had enough. That night I decided to go to the club. I was so annoyed by what I'd had to put my men through, that before I went to the club I removed the Engineer Castle insignia from my uniform collar, and replaced it with the chaplain's Insignia of the Cross.

I had a beer, thought about my family, career, and my next possible assignment. It so happened that some Red Cross ladies up from Seoul had been invited to the dedication. When they saw me sitting alone, they came over and asked if they could join the chaplain. I said sure. No sooner had I said sure then I noticed General Sands glaring at the chaplain's insignia that I was wearing. As I was leaving, the general's aide approached me and said that the CG has told him to inform me that I was to report to him after the dedication. He intended to use Article 15, which is an administrative reprimand where the target – me – would admit to committing a minor infraction. In the case of an officer, this can mean the end of his career. I knew that this mean the end of my career.

So off to my quarters and sack time. The guests at the dedication were Korean dignitaries, their generals, the U.S. ambassador, U.S. Generals, 7th Division senior commanders, Dan Raymond, and I, as a major who was in charge of the construction, was the junior officer invited.

I was also the last person in the receiving line. When my name was announced, General Sands shook my hand warmly, and said, "Ray you did a wonderful job of construction and clean up. Everything went as smooth as silk. You have made me very proud this day.

In response I said, "Sir, I am glad you are pleased. I have not forgotten that I'm to report to you at the conclusion of this important dedication day."

General Sands replied, "Oh yes, Ray forget that meeting.

I smiled and told him, "General, you don't know how pleased you have just made me."

He smiled back and I departed.

I'm not sure if Dan Raymond had talked with him, or if the general had realized how hard I had worked. He certainly was disappointed at the failure of his own people, and I just happened to be wearing the cross on my color and not my castle.

(An interesting note: General Sands, who was at one time going to administer Article 15 for wearing the Chaplain's Cross, later awarded me the 7th Division Certificate of Achievement.)

A little known incident to completely end the chapel story. During the chapel construction, many well-intentioned persons had their ideas about the non-denominational chapel, including those who never attended any church. One idea that won much verbal approval was the concept that not only should the Christian cross and the Star of David be available but we should display the Torii as well for the Korean soldiers. A Torii was constructed, and during its installation a crisis arose. That design was a Japanese type Torii. That symbol would be an affront to our 7th Division Korean soldiers. We quickly removed the incorrect unit, made a Korean Torii, and had it promptly installed in place This prevented what could have been a major embarrassment for all.

Lesson learned: Insist that all involved had to sign off on any verbal concept, design or change, regardless how well-meaning ideas are made. After official drawings are approved no changes will be accepted without a written order.

Additional accomplished missions during my time in Korea included the construction of rifle range, a water point, and road-base preparation for later black top paving in the division area.

Providing Entertainment

A well-known and respected military entertainer was the great comedic actor Bob Hope. During the Second World War, he would organize a military entertainment show of popular artists and performers. The show normally included a band or orchestra, comedians, and always very pretty young ladies who would sing. They would often select a bashful young man from the audience to come onto the stage, and they would sing a love song or other popular songs to the soldier...to the delight of all. Need I note that the female performers were scantily attired.

This background is provided for the children of the seventies since some of them are not familiar with these soldier shows.

Bob Hope continued his program in all the wars – no matter how the politicians described the operations. (They called the Korean War a "police action.") He and his troupes also entertained at military hospitals.

During my time in the 7th Division, the Bob Hope Show was scheduled to perform for our division. The key performers would visit the entertainment sight, meet the senior brass, and list the support that they would require. This particular show took place in the dead of winter. The female entertainers said that it was so ice cold that they could not perform in their normal brief attire, unless there was some way to heat the stage. Guess who got the job to figure out a way to heat the stage. Yep, me. You just don't want a division's worth of soldiers disappointed, nor the brass who would hear their complaints.

I understood that the U.S. Air Force had special heaters to warm jet engines in the most severe weather conditions. The Department of Defense had also advised senior commanders to support the Bob Hope Shows, since they were worthwhile morale boosters. So off I went to the airbase, and I invited their CO to our soldiers' show, explaining that I needed to borrow two Herman-Nelson jet engine heaters. When they arrived I positioned one heater so that its blast of warm air was directed across the stage towards the back drop curtain. The second heater was placed on the opposite side of the stage blowing warm air toward the first heater. It covered the microphone and the dancing area. Although the troop seats were mere sand bags, nobody complained about the cold.

7ᵗʰ Infantry Division Engineers First Korean Party

(Sponsored by 13ᵗʰ Engineer Combat Battalion)

One day at an operational meeting, my boss and good friend Lt. Col. Dan Raymond said that we had accomplished many engineer missions so well that we should institute an annual Bull Dozer Ball. Everyone present concurred. Then Dan said to me, "And Ray, what's a party without ladies. You as my Operations Officer will be responsible for providing the ladies."

There were no indigenous females allowed in the 7ᵗʰ Division area. And anyway, inviting these persons at that time was out of the question. Dan had already invited Gen. Sands, and the Assistant Division Commanding Officer(a one-star), all regimental commanders, and all other division brass.

The arrival of those guests was to be celebrated as follows:

    - A small bridge would be erected at the vehicle dismount point.

    - Two borrowed tanks equipped with search lights pointed skyward just like a Hollywood Premier would have their beams cross each other in the sky.

    - As guests arrived they would be greeted by battalion officers and escorted over the temporary bridge we had constructed for this event, and into our Battalion Officers Club.

- Kobe beef from Japan would be served and music provided after dinner.

The pressure was on me to provide ladies who were U.S. citizens, whom we referred to as "Round Eyes."

I asked all of the officers I knew if they had any ideas or leads to help me find ladies for the event. But we were all in the same situation. There was no help of any kind.

Finally, I realized that the 8th Army Headquarters and U.S. State Department had women working in Seoul many miles south of our Division. After some intelligence work, I obtained a Seoul Civilian-Military telephone directory that provided the telephone number with the name of the Civilian Civil Service Personnel Chief in Seoul and I called her. She said the long trip north on poor roads in an Army bus was of no interest to the ladies working in Seoul. She added that she was not nearly as young as the young women whose personnel records she managed, and she was not interested in sitting on the sidelines at a social event.

I noticed from her speech patterns and accent that she was from the Philadelphia area. Since I had been stationed in Philadelphia on National Guard Duty in previous years, I asked her to reconsider her decision. I added that should she provide the full bus of lady guests, that I would arrange a sedan with a driver for her transportation.

In addition, I told her that on her arrival, that Major Ramos would personally welcome her and that when the music started after dinner, he would dance every single dance that her feet could take. She then asked me to spell my name, which I did. At that point, an additional commitment was made to seal the deal, when I said that when she wished to rest her feet, Major Ramos would be at her side. It was then that she agreed to have the ladies attend our party en masse.

Little did she know what I did at the next Battalion Officers meeting. I announced that I was having sixty name tags made with the name Ramos inscribed. Each officer and male guest would also be given that name tag to wear at the party.

When her sedan arrived a young officer opened the door and extended our welcome. Her first words were, "Where is Major Ramos?"

At that I came forward saluted her and said, "Welcome to our party." A wonderful dinner was served, and musical entertainment and dancing followed. A real nice party. Dan Raymond was very pleased and all the brass and ladies enjoyed the evening. And "Ramos" kept his promise; he never left her side. (All the guys took turns.)

The weather in Korea was always unpredictable. That night one of the most severe snow storms hit us. All the roads were closed for traffic. The ladies were stranded. I talked with Dan, and we agreed to give the officers' sleeping quarters to our lady guests. I'm sure that Dan obtained Gen. Sands concurrence with our decision. Each officer remade his bed with clean sheets, and laundered pajamas, a new toothbrush and paste, soap, and a piece of chocolate candy was left on the pillow with a little note. None of us knew which lady would occupy which bed, so the note was addressed to "Our Dear Guest." An armed guard was posted at each door all night.

The next morning, after breakfast, the roads were clear, and we wished the ladies a safe trip back to Seoul.

At the next staff meeting, everyone discussed selecting the next date for the future Bull Dozer Ball. My rotation date was only a few months away, and I was pleased to know that some other operations officer would have to provide the ladies.

I must also say that throughout all of my trials and tribulations in Korea, my family was always on my mind.

Chief of Engineers - Liaison with Combat Development Experimentation Center (Washington, D.C.)

The Army Corps of Engineers is one of the four combat branches of the Army; the others being Infantry, Artillery, and Armor. The Corps also has a service or technical function like dredging to maintain na-vigable rivers and construction.

Each Army Technical Branch developed its own specialized equip-ment to satisfy the Army's overall requirements. While I was on this assignment, the testing and field evaluation of developmental equip-ment was conducted at Camp Roberts or the Hunter Liggett Military

Reservation in the vicinity of Jolon Junction, California. Prior to WWII a part of the neighboring William Randolph Hurst large family retreat estate was acquired by the federal government. Segments of it originally were adjacent to the old Franciscan Mission San Antonio of the California chain of missions.

The Corps of Engineers had the responsibility of developing a night vision apparatus that could take the sky ambient light on the darkest of nights and cascade or magnify that non-detectable human eye light against enemy personnel without emitting any originating signal to identify friendly tactical positioning, unlike a regular light.

My initial experience was with the first field concept unit which was so large that it was mounted on a heavy sturdy metal tripod. Field tests were providing excellent resolution results. However, it was far too bulky and much too heavy for troop use. Over the years, individual soldiers night vision equipment has now been developed for efficient attachment to the helmet. Its use is also employed by law enforcement, and, under certain requirements, by civilians.

Another interesting development was the thermograph which used body heat as a base marker. In development, it was bulky. However, in further refinement and availability of stronger lighter weight material, it has now evolved not only for military application but for use by law enforcement.

Many police helicopters have thermographs installed which give them the ability to see police suspects fleeing into wooded or commercial areas. The contrast of body temperature with the surrounding temperature determines the suspect's location. The military application is obvious.

My assignment was not only to report on engineer developments, but to be the on site eyes and ears of all field experiment recommendations to the three-star chief of engineers in Washington, D.C.

My actual direct boss was a one-star general who decided what information would be appropriate to forward to the three-star boss.

In my monthly reports, I included the monitoring of developmental and proposed operational employment of other services equipment.

At the Experimentation Center, I had colleagues from all other branches of the Army, the Marine Corps, as well as from the United

Kingdom and Canada.

As another example, the WWII Army Garand M-1 riffle was developed by Army Ordnance as a semi-automatic rifle requirement primarily for infantry use. Its testing and improvement had input not only from the Army but from the Marine Corps and Navy as well.

In the night vision and thermograph developments mentioned above, the Army obtained meaningful comments from the other impacted and interested agencies. When invited, certain allied organizations also provided observations. During development some of these items were highly classified.

One of the big benefits of working on these projects was that I was assigned to Ft. Ord, and living with my family in Carmel, California, not twenty minutes away. That was not to last

On to Paraguay...Two New Languages – Spanish and Guarani

Among the Latin American governments, there was a concept for many years that contemplated a highway from Alaska in the North to the Southern part of Argentina, a connection that would encourage trade and tourism and would result in benefits to all nations in the Western Hemisphere. Each country would be responsible for the construction of the route within its boarders.

At the time, I had been in receipt of alert orders to return to Europe for duty in occupied Germany. The family was delighted. We were at that time living in Carmel, but they had loved living in Austria.

One day I received a telephone call from the Engineer Career Branch in the Pentagon advising that my alert for Germany had been canceled, and that I was going to receive new orders assigning me to the U.S. Military Mission in Asuncion, Paraguay. I asked why the change. The answer was that I would be replacing an engineer lieutenant colonel.

When I talked about the change in orders with Grace, I explained that the entire family could accompany me on this assignment. She asked about schools, the military hospital, commissary, dental support, the major disruption on the family, Spanish language, and so many other issues. She said that she and the children would be able to communicate in German after living in Austria. However,

Spanish would be difficult since they were older now.

The assignment to Paraguay would be very upsetting for the children. They liked their schools and she would have to "home school" our children. She added that our daughter Kathy had a four-year scholarship to a prestigious all-girls high school that she would have to forfeit. After much evaluation with Grace, we declined the dependent element of the assignment; that is, I would be going, but my family would stay in the United States.

I did not then know why there had been the abrupt change of orders. In fact, once on station in Paraguay, I never even heard the name of the officer I was replacing, or anything about him. There was an unconfirmed rumor that there was a raft transporting a bulldozer over a stream when the young Paraguayan operating the raft got nervous. At the point of greatest velocity, he inadvertently shifted the tractor's center of gravity which caused the raft to flip over. The bulldozer hit my predecessor, and so there was the sudden need for a replacement. This is speculation on my part, and I never directly asked for verification from U.S. sources or from my Paraguayan officer friends.

From Ft. Ord, I telephoned some career people I knew in Washington, asking them how I was selected for such an assignment when I only knew one word in Spanish.

The action officer responded by reading the qualifications for the position: the replacement had to have a Hispanic surname, must be a Roman Catholic, under forty years of age, married, be an officer of the U.S. Army Corps of the Engineers, a CGSC graduate, and so on. It did not say that the Spanish language was a requirement.

The action officer said they were sending me to a place where I could "use my mother's tongue." I said that I was using my mothers tongue right then on the phone, and it was English.

When he heard that he said, "We sent your complete file through the State Department to the Paraguayan ambassador here in Washington. Their ambassador concurred with the choice and sent the file to the president of Paraguay who approved the assignment. We can't change it. Start taking instant Spanish pills now."

That remark was not meant to be a joke. He was stressing the urgency of the situation and my need to learn some Spanish.

The Army Language School, now called the Defense Language Institute, is located in Monterey only four miles south of Ft. Ord. All language instructors must have full command of the language they taught, and have complete speaking capacity of their subject. I explained my problem and they gave me special language tapes developed at the school.

My orders directed me first to proceed to Washington, D.C. for orientation, and from there I would be sent on to my duty station Asuncion, Paraguay.

After my stay in Washington, I flew commercially on Pan American Airlines, in uniform, with a first stop in Panama. On arrival there, I telephoned an old friend, Major Jack Ruby, who was stationed in Panama. (Not the Jack Ruby who shot Lee Harvey Oswald who had shot President Kennedy.) My friend Jack's wife had just died and he and his children, who were the same age as my own children, were grieving over the untimely loss.

Jack told me that he would pick me up in a few minutes. When he saw me in the uniform I had worn on my departure from California, he expressed surprise. I acknowledged the situation, telling Jack that the heat at the Panama Airport in the wool uniform was a real problem for me. Jack then told me that the temperature in Panama was cool compared to where I was going.

Jack asked me to say over night with him, saying that he needed to talk with me about how he might manage the loss of his wife, Ruth, with their kids. He also had me pack my uniform, and instead gave me an old golf shirt and pants of his to wear to my next stop in Buenos Aires, Argentina, from where I would fly on to Asuncion, the capital of Paraguay. He said that when I arrived there, that I should find a local hotel where I could shower, shave, and change into my white and cooler tropical uniform before I reported for duty. It sounded like a good idea.

The next day in Jack's somewhat stained golf clothes I departed on the next Pan Am flight. To better describe my attire, Jack was several inches shorter than I, so the bottom of the slacks were above my ankles and the shirt fit a bit tight. I thought that it would make no difference since I would report for duty in my proper uniform the day after I arrived.

After the Buenos Aires stop, the aircraft flew to Asuncion. During the landing procedure I could see soldiers lined up, and there was a band with flags. After the full stop, none of the plane's passengers were leaving their seats. Everyone was looking out of the windows to assess the situation. I wondered who the VIP could be. I decided to stay in my seat until the ceremony was completed, then find a taxi and have the driver take me to a local hotel.

But that is not what happened. A stewardess, in beautiful Spanish, said, "I believe that you are Lieutenant Colonel Ramos of the U.S. Army. All of that is for you."

I understood enough to know what she said. Then she said no one gets off this aircraft until your welcoming is completed.

When the door opened, the band began to play. A red carpet had been placed at the first step under the stairs to the plane. Then a Paraguayan general came up to me. He wore many medals and had a knife and ammunition showing, and said to me, in Spanish of course, "In the name of the President of the Republic of Paraguay and the Commander of its armed forces, welcome to Paraguay."

Then he saluted me and kissed me on each cheek. Never before in my life had I been kissed by another man. I thought, "Here I am looking like a lost soul. But thank God, my new boss is not here."

Wrong! To the rear of the Paraguayan entourage I noticed a U.S. Army colonel who looked madder than mad. After the welcome ceremony, he put me in the back seat of his car and began doing a job on me like no other. Finally, he said that I had embarrassed the U.S. government, the Army, the U.S. Ambassador, the officers, and so on. As we arrived at the hotel, he said, "Ramos, the only acceptable thing about you is that you are fluent in Spanish."

Not wanting to ignite another explosion, I remained silent. He then left me at the curb and he and his driver drove off.

That evening I had my uniform pressed and I shined my insignia like never before. The hotel owners spoke English, and I had them write a few phrases in Spanish for me to use when I was introduced the next morning at the president's palace. Things like, "Mr. President, I am very happy to be here." And, "Mr. President, I am anxious to work with your engineers for the good of Paraguay." "Mr. President, etc., etc."

Meeting the President

The next morning, my boss, with the U.S. Ambassador, took me to the palace. On arrival, there were guards everywhere. After shaking hands with the president, he introduced me to the leaders of the Army, Air Force, and the Chief of Engineers. Then we all took seats and the President said to me in Spanish, "You come from the powerful and great country of the north. But there is one place that we are equal. The United Nations. We each have one vote. I have instructed my ambassador to always support the U.S. position. The single exception would be if I told him to do otherwise. What do you think of that Col. Ramos?"

I looked at my note card and said, "Mr. President, I am very happy to be here." Then there was total silence. I had responded in poor Spanish and had not answered the President's question. Somehow we got through the ceremony.

Later, the U.S. ambassador told me that in addition to Spanish, the Guarani language of the indigenous Indians is proudly spoken by all Paraguayans. Then the president laughed and everybody joined in. He said we were equal in that condition. On hearing, that I made a mental note to learn some sentences in Guarani for use next time we met.

About Paraguay

During the time of our civil war (1861-1865), the Paraguayans were also at war in what was called the war of the Triple Alliance. They fought Brazil, Bolivia, and Argentina at the same time. The bulk of the bitter fighting took place in the Gran Chaco, a large uninhabitable swamp and jungle area. The population of their opponents was so large that the Paraguayan male population could not sustain the prolonged war. Their females took up the weapons of the fallen male soldiers to continue the fight. At long last, they lost the struggle.

My assistance and support was geared toward the construction of a main route to provide commerce between villages, and to open those areas for population growth. The government offered interior land to Soviet and Japanese refugees for colonization in that remote part of the nation. Both of these ethnic groups were very disciplined and ambitious.

After a few generations, they made a difficult and foreboding land become a "land of milk and honey." While I was there, I noticed that they had no police station or a jail, and these two groups married within their own ethnic kind. Their little towns flourished and provided wonderful fruits, and vegetables, and their excess produce was sold in the capital of Asuncion.

Paraguay had no national airline. Their only commercial airline service was provided by non-Paraguayan carriers to and from the capital with no internal service. The U.S. government provided Douglas DC-3 twin-engine propeller-driven commercial-type aircraft to maintain their flying skill. There were no combat aircraft. On occasion, I would have to fly into the interior to coordinate anticipated construction support. Since there was no commercial airline and the military pilots had need to maintain their flight proficiency, the government sold tickets to fly on their DC-3 airplanes to the public.

The DC-3 was similar to the aircraft used in WWII to drop paratroopers. The events of one flight are still very vivid in my memory. One day I went to the local dirt strip outside of a small village. The aircraft was already on the ground and passengers, who had been standing in line in the hot sun for some time, were getting on board. Some were bringing pigs (for slaughter), chickens in boxes, eggs in crates, and agricultural products. I did not go to the line of passengers because I knew that the pilot would take me immediately to the front to be seated.

When everyone was aboard, he checked for my seat and found that the plane was completely full of Paraguayans and cargo. He told me to follow him into the cabin. There he told the co-pilot to wait for the next flight, and he put me in the co-pilot's seat.

I noticed that several gauges were missing from the instrument panel, and I asked him how he could fly without these gauges. He looked at me, smiled, and said that when the gauges were out of calibration or they no longer worked it was better to simply remove them. The co-pilot kicked the tires (I guess for good luck), the pilot made the sign of the cross, and we took off for the capital where we arrived safely.

Generally, each month I would return to the capital and write a status report for my boss. The other officers who worked with the infantry, artillery, and other Army components did the same. While in Asuncion, I met the local Franciscan priest who enlisted our help in building basic little houses for the poor. We obtained the support of General Careaga, their army chief of engineers, to use bulldozers, graders, and other equipment and supplies to further this very worthy project.

Routine scheduling of maintenance for heavy equipment was a concept not easy to achieve in a country where modern construction machines were just being introduced, and into an inhospitable environment. Where they needed, but didn't get, regular and heavy maintenance. Equipment lubrication points were promptly covered with mud and dust. On a scheduled basis, they must have all dried mud and dust wiped clean before injecting grease into the bearings (or oil in the case of an air filter).

Since those machines were a gift (in lieu of fighter jets and tanks) of the U.S. taxpayers. In a diplomatic way I tried to get compliance with maintenance needs, but without much success. One day in General Careaga's office, I suggested that he accompany me on the job unannounced. He agreed. Generals do not put their hands in oil or grease. At the site, I stopped a dozer as it was working on the job. I climbed up on the machine and offered my hand to the general. I always called him "my boss."

Once on the tractor with many of his officers standing by, I removed the cover from the oil bath cleaner. I said to General Careaga, "With your permission, sir..." And I took his hand in mine and put our hands in the fluid to the bottom. It was full of a mixture of oil, sticky black sand, and grit. He was shocked. The result of that trip solved, for the most part, the problem of a lack of maintenance.

On this job, as the road progressed, I needed new temporary "quarters." My new house was constructed of local materials by a man named Ramos. I jokingly called him my cousin. He did a great job and the roof never leaked. As the job progressed, and we were further away from my house, it was abandoned, and Mr. Ramos built a new replacement unit for me. At times the U.S. embassy would send a person to take photos, ask questions, and write a story for the local Spanish newspapers telling the population how the U.S. was helping in their modernization goals.

While establishing a route center line for clearing crews to follow, out of the thick jungle came two nude indigent Indian Guarani women. They were all painted and one of them had wrapped around her body, the largest, longest most menacing snake you can imagine. They spoke to me only in Guarani. They said that they had a special gift for me. The one not wearing the snake began to unwrap from her friend and then she tried to wrap the thing around me! I explained that my President Kennedy did not permit his soldiers to have pets. I was very sorry but I had to return their gift. And I hate snakes.

At the conclusion of the snake gift episode, I noticed a group Guarani men back in the woods behind trees with spears, bow and arrows, and other strange looking weapons, all focused intently on my action. It was a big, big stretch to think of my new "friends" as ladies. No offense intended since their diet, lifestyle, customs and traditions were so completely different from ours. I treated them with respect.

Dining at the Ritz

The Paraguayan Army food ration provided in the Gran Chaco jungle between Brazil and Paraguay was a world away from the U.S. troop field ration. Their food served for breakfast, lunch, and dinner came out of the same pot. It was the exact same food.

The food container was a former 55-gallon fuel drum cut in half with iron handles welded to both sides. The food in the pot was rice, meat from a locally-hunted wild animal, and local surface water. The pot was positioned over a wood fire pit where it cooked the contents for hours. The boiling (theoretically) eliminated any bacteria.

While in the learning "food appreciation phase," I ate their food out of necessity. On my return to the capital, I had the U.S. Air Force attaché bring back from Panama, cases of canned food like beans, soups, pork and beans, stew and the like, along with saltine crackers and whatever would travel. I planned to conceal enough of that food in the vehicle for each field period.

My food option was working well. At the noon meal time, I would disappear, taking my rations, and go some distance from the mess area and into the woods to eat my food from the can. One day a Paraguayan lieutenant found me. He said, "My colonel, you are eating American Food. I never had American food. It must be very good."

I knew he was asking for a can which I gave him. I said to him, "This is a big secret. I know that I can trust you."

He said, "Of course, sir."

Guess what. The very next day he was back with a friend.

It wasn't long before all my rations were gone and I was back to the pot.

So much for keeping secrets.

I was provided with a Paraguayan ID card and had dual status. In our army, I was a lieutenant colonel, but in their army I was one grade higher, a full colonel. The only Paraguayan military people that out ranked me were their generals.

At the completion of the work in Paraguay, I was assigned again back home to Ft. Ord. This time as chief of a Field Experimentation Team working with scientists from Stanford University.

Dominican Revolution

In May of 1965, Fidel Castro sent Cuban troops with arms into the poorest areas of the Dominican Republic. They promised the peasants medical care, work, and generally better living conditions if they would participate in the overthrow of the existing government. The Cubans said that the Dominican government oppressed the poor.

If people are poor, pretty much unemployed with little or no education, and they receive great promises, they could certainly be recruited to rebel, especially when they were supplied with weapons. The revolution soon ensued. The communists "promise"of a better tomorrow, e.g., that all Dominicans would be financially equal, and other propaganda, put the locally-elected government in grave peril. President Lyndon Johnson was told that embassies and foreign nationals could not be protected.

The revolution was going very badly for the Dominican government troops. Their president telephoned President Johnson saying if he didn't send U.S. troops in by the next day, the nation will fall and become the first "domino theory" country to succumb to communism in that part of the world.

U.S. troops arrived the next day. At the same time, the Organization of American States activated their military arm identified as the Inter-American Peace Force (IAPF). Troops were from Costa Rica, Honduras, Nicaragua, Paraguay, as well as from the United States. More than half the troops came from the U.S.

President Johnson did not want it to appear that the U.S. was using the "Big Stick Policy." Accordingly, a Brazilian four-star general named Braga was appointed to command the Inter-American Force with a three-star U.S. general as his deputy commanding general. (I took my meals in the Brazilian general's mess. All of the allied officers were fond of him.) A colonel from Nicaragua was the chief of staff.

My role in this multi-national force was that of the Command Engineer of the IAPF. During the period of fighting, there was significant damage to facilities, bridges, water, sewage, and the need to remove some 600 tons of debris. These and many other engineer tasks were accomplished by U.S. engineer troops.

When the conventional fighting was over, the communists resorted to sabotage. We provided portable safe water points with signs in both Spanish and English saying "Safe Drinking Water Courtesy of the IAPF." Then we discovered that Mr. Castro's "friends" had put dead rats in the 3000-gallon portable tanks. That meant cleaning the tanks and posting armed guard.

After the fighting was over, everyone still wore a .45-caliber pistol when leaving the headquarters on business or to inspect a construction job. That imposed a requirement that all officers had to go to the pistol range and qualify to properly handle and fire the pistol. In planning for that qualification, I decided that the general should open the range by firing the first shot. I obtained a target and made the bull's eye larger. I then rolled a very thin plastic string of Composition "C" plastic explosive and attached an electrical firing system to my circular fabricated charge. From the rear of the target, the explosive looked somewhat like a thin circular piece of spaghetti.

I tested the idea and it worked just fine. On the day of the general's firing the opening shot I stood behind him. There were 35 officers from his headquarters all at the opening to observe the general dedicating the pistol range. The general stepped up to his marked spot, loaded his pistol, took careful aim, and pulled the trigger. At that exact moment, I fired the charge that blew a hole in the bull's eye with a diameter of about three feet. Right away he turned, looked at me and said, "I know you did that."

Everybody clapped and cheered. I told General Braga that he was such an expert he should be exempt from any further familiarization firing. All concurred.

Shortly thereafter there were elections and the Dominican People picked a new democratic government. Accordingly, the IAPF was disbanded and all of the troops returned to their own countries. From there I was assigned to Ft. Benning, Georgia.

The Infantry Center, Ft. Benning, Georgia

After completing my assignment in the Dominican Republic, I was selected to command the 43rd Engineer Construction Battalion's activation, organization, and training for development.

The opportunity for Engineer Command is very limited due to the small number of engineer battalions. The Ft. Benning Infantry Center is the heart and soul of the Army's infantry training component. Other combat branches provide battalions there like artillery and armor to support infantry training and demonstrate to future infantry leaders the proper employment of their branch assets. Again, I was most fortunate.

On assuming command, I had the Battalion Operations Officer brief me on the various projects assigned and their status. At the conclusion of that meeting I asked why there was no mention of quarry rock production? The answer provided was that there were no igneous rock formations in the area, and for that reason the rock-crushing plant had never been used. I found that an unacceptable answer and said so.

I arranged the same day for a helicopter to fly me on an aerial reconnaissance. The pilot flew in concentric circles. After hours of using this technique, I spotted what looked like an old abandoned quarry adjacent to a county road. On return I had the contracting officer at Ft. Benning headquarters determine who were the property owners, and to arrange a lease. When those administrative tasks were completed, we then needed to pump out the water from the quarry, do the necessary clean up, and promptly begin quarry operations in support of Ft. Benning.

In addition to the rock-crushing plant, this battalion also had 25 five-ton capacity dump trucks, fifteen D-9 bulldozers, bucket loaders, road graders, generators for continuous night operations, and different caliber weapons. When the rock-crusher plant went into production, the various senior staff officers and commanders, including a two-star engineer general from the east coast, all came to Ft. Benning to observe this newly activated 43rd Engineer Battalion.

A "Can Do" Attitude

From time to time, I heard the word "can't" used as an excuse for potential delay or noncompliance. These soldiers (about 1,500) and officers each in their own way might be testing the commanding officer like what had occurred in the Austrian situation many years earlier. At the next staff meeting I said that the word "can't" hereafter will not be used or tolerated in this battalion. The attitude will be "can do." I also initiated reveille as in my former commands where all personnel attended. While I myself did not have to attend, I did anyway.

With a new attitude, tasks began to manifest themselves. We had a number of soldiers skilled in brick, stone, block work, carpentry, structural design, heavy equipment operation, asphalt, concrete, drafting, engineering, drawing, and related skills. About the same time we had the opportunity to do some road rehabilitation and asphalt work. Before undertaking those types of work, I had to be certain that soldier labor and equipment involved would not negatively impact local union work or any type of civilian labor enterprise. The road selected was a county dirt road to Ft. Benning and used primarily by off-post military and Ft. Benning civilian employees.

There was no county priority or funding for this road in the foreseeable future Not only did this training benefit our soldiers, Ft. Benning employees, military living off-post, and residents living along this road, but now their former traffic dust problem had been eliminated.

Another training construction operation that exercised equipment and offered other specialized soldier training was a bridge that gave vehicle access to the paratroop drop zone. After airborne training drops, all of that equipment had to be recovered, delivered for inspection, repaired when warranted, re-packed, and made ready for the next parachute jump.

When the bridge was completed and in use, Ft. Benning had a visitor whose name was John Wayne. Yes, the famous movie actor. The Green Berets soldiers were much admired by the public, and Mr. Wayne had authorization from the Pentagon to provide him with as much support as he needed in the making of his movie about the Green Beret soldiers.

The movie title during the Vietnam war was only three words "The Green Berets." It's story line was about John Wayne and his Green Beret team who capture a notorious North Vietnamese general in his own headquarters, and bring him to South Vietnam to be tried for war crimes. A major scene in the film was a chase by the North Vietnamese general's security guard detailed to free him from his captors and to kill the Green Berets.

During Mr. Wayne's reconnaissance of the Ft. Benning training sites, he traveled over our bridge. He said, "Ah, here is the exact bridge we want to destroy in the chase scene."

There was no point making objections or suggesting another bridge. For the movie, the Hollywood set design people, strung moss with paint and other magic, made our bridge look the part. During the filming they blew up our bridge, and they funded its replacement.

Draftees

During the Vietnam "conflict," the draft provided significant numbers of young men for eventful service in Southeast Asia. Whenever I had a few spare moments, I would go to the reception area where draftees would arrive for duty. They came by train and bus. The drill sergeant would identify the first 40, assigning each man a number. Then that group would start their induction process.

There was a nearby building with an entry door in view. The exit door at the other end was not visible. The first forty men would pass through the entry door, and then it would close. Those men found themselves in a forty-chair barber shop. Most of the recruits had long hair. The barber would say something like, "Sir, how would you like your hair cut today?"

Some recruits would say something like, "Maybe just a trim around the edges." Then the clippers were energized and long thick hair began to fall to the floor. In two or three minutes all heads were very close cut.

In the next building, they were issued boots, underwear and fatigues (work uniforms). Twelve weeks later, in a parade, they would have become soldiers, with orders. A proud event for all to see.

Team Building

One of my important goals was the continued development of morals and leadership qualities on the part of officers and NCOs. There were many ways to achieve that goal. Here are two examples.

One of my black lieutenant's wife had just given birth to their first baby at the post hospital. I went to see her at the maternity ward. I had removed my hat and it just happened to cover my name, when the chief nurse saw me. She told me that she was sorry but only the husband could visit the wife. It was a matter of policy and protection for mothers and babies.

I told the chief nurse that the new mother was my wife.

Her response, as she minimized her surprise, was, "Of course, sir, please follow me."

At the young woman's bedside, I put my cheek next to hers and asked her how was she feeling, and how was her little daughter doing. She, of course, knew the hospital policy, and I knew that when her real husband came that night to visit, that she would be telling him what happened. And he would be telling the other black officers what I did, in showing my interest in his wife and their baby.

Another example...once, when passing the post commissary on the way to verify the progress on the various jobs, I saw the wife of one of my NCOs exiting the store with a large shopping cart of food while she was trying to control a couple of active little ones.

I had my driver stop the jeep. I greeted the lady, saluted her, and took the cart to her car. My driver took the oldest child and the lady the youngest. I knew that night she would tell the husband what had transpired that day. It was about building unity and Army esprit de corps

These were just a couple of examples of how I worked to build loyalty, army commitment, morale, respect, and family values among my men, because I knew these qualities made for a strong organization of camaraderie in combat. Battalion evening officers classes and NCO training were also used to increase professional standards.

Civil Service

In competition with other nations for many years, the Army has produced some of the number one rifle teams in the world. A new road was needed to support this training and eventual competitions. The 43rd Engineers planned a system to maximize the equipment capabilities, and bring the new access road to completion on schedule.

Activating and training a highly technical military organization with an eventual strength in excess of 1,000 men is a significant task. When available, the utilization of experienced government Civil Service technicians with our NCOs can greatly increase heavy equipment operators productivity. It also reduces the incidence of unintentional equipment mishandling and timely receipt of manufacturing warnings or defects.

Worldwide, the Army had some 1,500 Civil Service engineer equipment technical employees. All major U.S. military bases had these office detachments as well as did friendly countries.

Ft. Benning had one of these detachment offices provided by the U.S. Army Mobility Equipment Command (MECOM) headquarters in St. Louis. At Ft. Benning, the only engineer battalion troop organization was the 43rd Engineers. Until its activation, this Civil Service detachment had very little work to do other than support some field power generating units, compasses, and other minor equipment.

Due to the complexity of equipment like a rock-crushing plant, significant numbers of large construction machines, an engineer lathe shop truck, survey and ancillary equipment, I arranged for the local MECOM Civil Service technicians to observe and assist our equipment operators in their training. That occurred on two or three occasions. However, when the weather turned cold, or during the winter rains, they had to test power generators or inspect compasses. Our soldiers trained and worked in rain, mud, heat, dust, and cold weather. I then wrote a complaint letter through technical channels to their MECOM headquarters. After that letter, there was a significant attitude improvement.

Promotion to the Grade of Colonel

One day nine months later, I was called to the commanding general's office, General Robert H. York. I was aware that a promotion from lieutenant colonel to colonel was in the works for me, but not when it would be announced. This was it.

General York pinned on me the very same eagles that had been used and given to him when he was promoted to full colonel years earlier. Those eagles were more detailed than those available today. I still have them.

At the same time, General York was being promoted to a Lieutenant General (three stars). He would be leaving Ft. Benning to command the Airborne Corps at Ft. Bragg, North Carolina, on the same day that I was going to my new command in St. Louis.

The continued war in Vietnam caused the government to increase the army size. Ft. Benning was going to have an engineer group activated and trained there. My 43rd Engineer Battalion would be a major subordinate unit of the group. An engineer group could likely have two combat engineer battalions and a number of specialized separate engineer companies for a total strength of about 3,000 officers and men commanded by a colonel, which was comparable to an Army brigade.

When the Engineer Group was to be activated, I had just been promoted, and General York wanted me to command that organization.

I received a call from the Pentagon Officers Career Branch saying that I had commanded a platoon, and later a company, and had just completed the command of a premier engineer battalion. I had more command experience than most engineer officers. They said since I had been recommended by a now famous three-star airborne general, they were in no position to repost me against his recommendation.

However, I was told that I would be denying another engineer colonel who may have little troop duty. He said, "We have another difficult assignment for a colonel that is a perfect fit for what you have done. If you will tell General York that your career branch has recommended a challenging assignment for you, he would likely concur."

Then in a very nice way the Career Branch officer, whom I knew said, "Ray should you not speak to General York along the lines of this call, on another day you will be up for another assignment, and we'll be here."

I knew that he was morally right and I accepted his comments.

Guess where the new orders sent me. Yep, to the Army Mobility Equipment Command (MECOM), St. Louis. I smiled and thought about the civilian technicians at Ft. Benning who told me that they had to inspect some compasses! Now I was going to be their boss...Ha!

What an Exit

Ironically, it happened that General York and I had selected the very same day to leave Ft. Benning, and almost at the same time. I had made plans for my jeep driver to put my two items of luggage on the rear seat and to take me to the commercial airport. I certainly had not coordinated my departure with a new three-star general.

After driving around in the area of my former command for the last look, we entered the main Ft. Benning road that one takes when leaving that large military base. I immediately noticed soldiers lined up with their weapons almost shoulder to shoulder. It was a sign of respect and to wish General York a safe trip to his new command. As the jeep approached each unit or different organization their officers would call attention! Then there was the order to give the rifle salute, with officers rendering the traditional hand salute.

My jeep had entered that reserved or temporarily closed road from an area side road. I am sure that the initial units officers had been told that the only vehicle approaching them would have General York as the passenger and that they would render the salute courtesy as previously rehearsed.

I realized of course that all that pomp and ceremony was not intended for me. I just happened to be on the right road at the right time. I returned hundreds of salutes. I also suspect that my driver knew that the main road had been reserved and closed from post headquarters to its connection with the civilian highway.

What an exit.

Mobility Equipment Command--St. Louis

Having written a letter concerning poor civilian technical support provided my battalion by the U.S. Army Mobility Equipment Command when I was activating and training my organization, I now found myself assigned to run the very same major organization that I had criticized about a year earlier.

Possibly the Army thought they'd like to see if Ramos could fix it. On reporting, I received a warm welcome from the Commanding General, another two-star. He explained that I was now the Director of Maintenance for all types of engineer equipment throughout the Army. I would use the various Army depots and civilian plants when Army rebuild shop space was overloaded to meet operational requirements. The directorate had no military personnel, but my deputy, the General said, was a very dedicated and competent Civil Service employee.

The Commanding General reminded me that with my skilled work force, I was now responsible for providing civilian technicians, and developing and identifying the parts that have a high or low mortality maintenance life.

The purpose was to anticipate what repair needs should be anticipated and what spare parts should be purchased by the Army and pre-positioned in the Army rebuild depots, both in the U.S. and overseas. The equipment included all sizes of bulldozers, road graders, air compressors, power generators, rock-crushing plants, water purification equipment, Army hospital train, all Army vessels, bridging equipment, and river and harbor dredging vessels. If it was construction or engineer type equipment, I was responsible for it, even small items like the compass (chuckle), in order to accomplish those multitude functions.

The Directorate was composed of 1,500 Civil Service Employees. I was the only military. I had skilled engineers, highly-experienced maintenance mechanics and the like. An all-civilian Civil Service work force.

That took me out of my soldiers army. I had to deal with Civil Service Regulations, all types of personnel issues, labor unions, and overtime rules to mention a few.

My assignment required that I would travel to various military head-quarters and civilian contractor facilities that were rebuilding combat damaged equipment from Vietnam and other parts of the world. From time to time I would have politicians asking about sending work to their congressional districts. Military officers from overseas commands would meet with me to request a higher priority or re-duced waiting time for urgently needed machines from rebuild shops. I also had to travel to Washington, D.C. to conduct various briefings.

I should also mention a policy in the Army Rebuild Depot System that no re-manufactured items would be released if not in 100% "like new" condition.

After an initial adjustment of working with Civil Service employees and their understanding of my commitment to the soldiers army, we came together for the common good. Possibly my uniform worn daily in their presence gave them a physical reminder as to why we were there.

In the Army, the soldier has no forty-hour contract, no guarantee of holidays off from duty. We belonged to Uncle Sam 24/7/365. I relied on my civilian deputy who brought me up to speed on the Civil Service world and overseas technical offices. I addressed the less than desirable relationships at some installations, advising them to take a new and more positive attitude in supporting our customer – The American Soldier. They knew if service did not improve, I could abolish their job or transfer them back to my headquarters.

During the Vietnam operations, among the many construction tasks performed by bulldozer operators was the preparation of helicopter landing pads on hillsides, in direct support of ongoing combat operations. The pads had to be of such size that helicopter blades would not strike the hill's upside. At times, that could be very demanding work.

Due to the operational urgency unfortunately, some dozer operators worked on the periphery of those elevated pads, resulting in traction loss, followed by a rollover causing the operator's ejection and subsequent serious injury or death.

When I heard of those types of tragedies, I ordered our engineering staff to immediately begin the design and testing of a safety cage type kit with an operator harness to reduce or hopefully eliminate those injuries and deaths.

During my tenure I also recognized the critical need to support operations in Vietnam which was used to clear brush, small trees and other terrain features that provided concealment for the enemy. With excellent concealment, the enemy could over-run our gunners.

Our rubber tired equipment was sorely needed to clear those "fields of fire." When requisitioned however, the overseas logistical and supply personnel could only issue a piece of paper saying when the machines arrive from the U.S. by boat, the request will be satisfied. This gave me great concern. This was my problem to solve quickly.

In reply to my questioning, more than enough units were ready for shipment of these machines, except for a lack of fenders! The manufactures with the contract for fender production was gearing up to fulfill his contract. "Gearing up" would not satisfy the soldier in Vietnam manning a machine gun pointed into brush at night.

I ordered the depots to find a substitute that could be used as fenders. Answer: There were no substitutes. I knew they had a lot of large conveyor belts used to support rock-crushers. I told them to cut the conveyor belts into required lengths, bolt them to the machines and ship the units the same day. My plan worked.

I was fortunate in having a very dedicated civilian deputy who shared my "can do/will do" policy. The St. Louis Civil Service skilled staff worked in a former WWII ammunition plant. The interior walls had not been painted since the conclusion of the First World War. Lighting for draftsmen, artists, and persons writing technical data for manuals, and the Preventative Service (PM) cartoon Soldiers Magazine had been sadly neglected. I obtained the funds to correct that problem. With the improvement of their work environment, their productivity significantly increased. Money well spent. That improvement was recognized as a surprise for me by those talented employees in the form of some cartoons at my farewell dinner.

My secretary, a happily married grandmother, was a great lady and a jewel who would stay after the regular work day to complete a briefing paper, verify budget requirements, consolidate depot repair parts requests, or complete a report. She declined overtime or compensatory time off. Her husband was also retiring and they worked for different employers. They wanted to be near their grandchildren. I hated to see her leave after working for me during the past two years.

I needed a well-groomed, professional, and smart secretary. As the director's secretary, her salary was several grades higher than that of a division chief's secretary. I wanted to select my replacement secretary from within the organization. Each qualified applicant was given a two-week familiarization or trial period. Based on performance, a selection would be made. Four of the five were married and in the 35 to 50 age group. They all scored well. The fifth and final candidate was a young woman in her early 20s.

I should mention that at times, senior officers having assignments similar to mine, supporting other equipment like helicopters, tanks, and artillery would meet with me to solve logistic issues of a common interest. I shared my fender shortage and use of fabricated rubber fenders to release equipment in depot for immediate shipment as an example. As was customary for these meetings, which could last for hours, we would take a break, and I'd have my secretary bring in coffee and light snacks.

I'll never forget one Monday morning I had scheduled a meeting with a visitor from Vietnam. Just before closing time on Friday, my deputy alerted the last woman competing for the secretarial job to be sure to have the snacks and coffee ready for the next work day. That Monday morning, our overseas guest arrived, and at break time I asked my deputy to have our secretary bring in some refreshments.

In came "Miss Lovely," dressed in a way I'd never seen before. She was wearing pants that accentuated her shape, and a tight fitting blouse with a low V that ended somewhat above her naval I guessed. This was her first time that she served snacks. Pouring coffee she seemed to be resting her bosom on the guest's shoulder. Obviously, she did not realize that the visitor nor I had any interest in looking at her charms. She never was promoted during my three years there.

Back to California

After three years in St. Louis, I was fortunate to be assigned as the Military Post Commander of Camp Roberts, California less than a half hours drive from Paso Robles and 90 minutes to Carmel. In my previous Ft. Ord experience I had been assigned officially to the Office, Chief of Engineers in Washington, D.C., and my observations, recommendations and reports were transmitted there. As you will remember, my boss was a brigadier general there as well.

I was their eyes on the ground at test sights at Camp Roberts, and Hunter Liggett Military Reservation.

This new job assignment, however, had me working for, and responsible for, field experimentation of certain operational capabilities, transportation, and potential employment of equipment.

To insure impartial validity of reported events, the Experimentations Center contracted with Stanford's Research Institute (SRI) to oversee and concur in the collection of technical field data and of the final written report. The field work and its reporting are beyond the scope of this book. One reminder and souvenir of that work was the awarding of SRI's Plaque designation, conferring on me their title of Senior Instant Engineer. It's duration was a two years assignment.

Camp Roberts is a 45,000-acre, military reservation that is bisected by Highway 101 located some eight miles north of Paso Robles. During WWII, it was at one time the training base for the 7th Infantry Division. For entertainment the United Service Organization (USO) hosted performances at Camp Roberts featuring such stars as Bob Hope, Jerry Colona, Dinah Shore, and Bing Crosby, along with many other talented Americans. In those days the Camp Roberts USO Soldiers Shows would have 15,000 to 20,000 troops in attendance.

This base had heavy maintenance repair shops to service tanks and other specialized equipment. Stored there was a complete MASH Hospital for deployment, if and when needed. Roberts had two paved air strips,187 miles of roads, 24,000 track feet of railroad,1,285 structures including barracks, mess halls, supply and administrative buildings, weapons firing ranges and field bivouac areas.

A separate Army Space Command specialized satellite communications tracking station was also permanently located at Camp Roberts. This military post has served Army requirements for WWII, Korea, Regular Army troop training from Ft. Ord, Combat Developments Classified Field Experiments, and all facilities for the California National Guard summer field training exercises.

During the Vietnam period, a concept was developed to have the thousands of infantry soldiers living west of the Mississippi River be trained at Camp Roberts, and after leave, they would be air lifted to Vietnam from Travis Air Force Base, northeast of San Francisco. Those from the east of the Mississippi would continue to be Ft. Benning trained. Obviously, a savings in time and money for the potential Camp Roberts soldiers.

With Richard Nixon's campaign promises, to gradually withdraw from Vietnam, and to reduce the overall armed force size and budget, the former East-West Infantry Training concept was no longer considered. The pressure to reduce the overall Department of Defense costs resulted in Camp Roberts also being identified as a base to be scheduled for closing.

As the Base Military Commander, I worked with local city officials, as well as with the press, state entities, civic, religious and citizen officials. I fully enjoyed my last military career year.

At a formal ceremony on April 2, 1971, I turned Camp Roberts over to the California National Guard Commanding General. Regular Army officials, state, county, city, local dignitaries, the press, including TV stations, attended.

At the base closing ceremony, I was presented with the artillery brass shell casing that fired the last salute round while under federal jurisdiction. My name is engraved on the shell case. Ronald Reagan, then the Governor of California, had a state memento plaque presented to me that day. The National Guard also gave me a key to the main reservation gate with an invitation to return anytime as their guest. When I departed the reservation later that day, I never returned since I was then about to begin a new civilian life at the end of my military career.

A New Life

After my retirement in 1971, I met a lady, Meredith J. Littleon, who had been born in San Francisco and had never married. We became friends, and after a year, we were married on July 7, 1973, in the Army Presidio of San Francisco Chapel. Meredith worked for a large industrial paper company known as the Crown Zellerbach Corporation. They had numerous mills and extensive tree farms in the Pacific Northwest, and plants in Holland, Brazil, and throughout the United States.

When management operated their mills during union strikes, Meredith worked in one of their laboratory facilities in product quality control. She also managed one of the company's component elements in the San Francisco corporate headquarters. She retired from Crown Zellerbach in 1985 after a 30-year career.

We both enjoyed living and working in the San Francisco Bay Area. In 1974, we purchased an oceanfront lot on property known as Belvedere Island across the Golden Gate in Marin County. During the inital Spanish explortation period when the Conquistadors (conquerors) began building the Presidio (fortress) of San Francisco, Belvedere was completely surrounded by water. In later years, a two city block long causeway from the city of Tiburo connected Belvedere to the mainland. Our first residence was there with two of the four survey points in San Francisco Bay with an unobstructed view of the city, Treasure Island, the East Bay Bridge, and the towers of the Golden Gte Bridge. We lived there for fourteen years.

During our marriage, Meredith designed and I did the survey as well as working on five homes. Every one was to be the house we would occupy until we passed away. None was built as a spec house to make a profit. The other locations were the Carmel Highlands on the ocean side of Highway One (Pacific Coast Highway), the Quail Meadows Country Club, the Pasadera (stepping stone) Country Country Club off Highway 68 in Monterey, and Bayview Estates in Kona, Hawaii where we now reside.

As this book goes to print, I am still active in my 94th year of life, and Meredith is enjoying life in her mid-eighties. God has been good to us. We pray each day for our loved ones, and ask God to bless our beautiful United States of America.

Final Words

Dear Children,

Your mother, Grace, an only child, had a little innocent childlike chuckle when she encountered humorous and intriguing situations. She always loved babies and early in our marriage she said that as an only child, she very much missed not having siblings to know, love, and grow up with. As a teenager and young lady, she never learned to cook since her parents were both good cooks. When married, however, she quickly got recipes and obtained ideas and guidance from her mother, Mrs. Hardy. I called Mrs. Hardy "Tiney" or "Nana."

When I first met Toodie, she was a senior in an all-girls Catholic high school Her favorite nun and teacher was Sister Rose of Mary. Many years later, she named our third daughter, Rosemary, after Sister Rose.

Your Mom was five-foot-five tall, blonde, and pretty. She was a wonderful dancer and very popular with her classmates. By the time that I entered the Army, we had become good friends. We also said that if I returned after the war uninjured, we would like resume dating. At that time we both lived in our parents homes.

Other books from Seton Publishing

Mokki's Peak - Tony Seton
Silent Alarm - Tony Seton
Deki-san - Tony Seton
Equinox - Tony Seton
Paradise Pond - Tony Seton
Selected Writings - Tony Seton
The Brink - Tony Seton
Jennifer - Tony Seton
The Francie LeVillard Mysteries - Volumes I thru VIII - Tony Seton
Trinidad Head - Tony Seton
Dead as a Doorbell - Tony Seton
Just Imagine - Tony Seton
Musings on Sherlock Holmes - Tony Seton
No Soap, Radio - Tony Seton
The Autobiography of John Dough, Gigolo - Tony Seton
Silver Lining - Tony Seton
Mayhem - Tony Seton
The Omega Crystal - Tony Seton
Truth Be Told - Tony Seton
The Quality Interview / Getting it Right
    on Both Sides of the Mic - Tony Seton
From Terror to Triumph / The Herma Smith Curtis Story -
    Tony Seton
Don't Mess with the Press / How to Write, Produce, and
    Report Quality Television News - Tony Seton
Right Car, Right Price - Tony Seton
Life Is a Bumpy Road - Tony Albano
From Hell to Hail Mary / A Cop's Story - Frank DiPaola
From Colored Town to Pebble Beach /
    The Story of the Singing Sheriff - Pat DuVal
The Early Troubles - Gerard Rose
The Boy Captain - Gerard Rose
Bless Me Father - Gerard Rose
For I Have Sinned - Gerard Rose
A Western Hero - Gerard Rose
Red Smith in LA Noir - David Jones
The Shadow Candidate - Rich Robinson
Hustle is Heaven - Duncan Matteson
Vision for a Healthy California - Bill Monning
Three Lives of a Warrior - Phil Butler
Live Better Longer - Hugh Wilson
Green-Lighting Your Future /
    How You Can Manifest the Perfect Life - John Koeberer

Made in the USA
San Bernardino, CA
05 September 2016